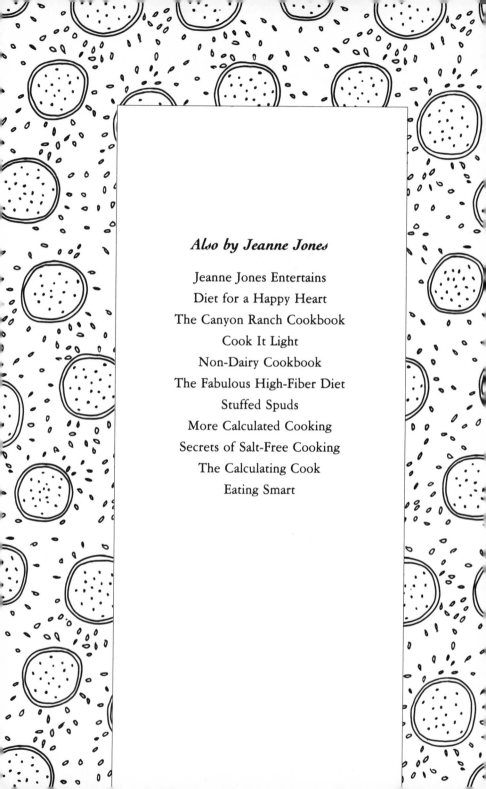

Also by Jeanne Jones

Jeanne Jones Entertains
Diet for a Happy Heart
The Canyon Ranch Cookbook
Cook It Light
Non-Dairy Cookbook
The Fabulous High-Fiber Diet
Stuffed Spuds
More Calculated Cooking
Secrets of Salt-Free Cooking
The Calculating Cook
Eating Smart

Eating
SMART

ABCs of the New Food Literacy

Jeanne Jones

Foreword by Antonio M. Gotto, Jr.,
M.D., D.Phil.

Preface by Lynne W. Scott,
M.A., R.D./L.D.

Macmillan Publishing Company
New York

Maxwell Macmillan Canada
Toronto

Maxwell Macmillan International
New York   Oxford   Singapore   Sydney

Macmillan Publishing Company
866 Third Avenue, New York, NY 10022

Maxwell Macmillan Canada, Inc.
1200 Eglinton Avenue East, Suite 200
Don Mills, Ontario M3C 3N1

Macmillan Publishing Company is part of the Maxwell Communication Group of Companies.

Library of Congress Cataloging-in-Publication Data
Jones, Jeanne.
    Eating smart: the ABCs of the new food literacy/Jeanne Jones.
        p.   cm.
    Includes index.
    ISBN 0-02-559772-8
    1. Nutrition.   2. Health—Nutritional aspects.   I. Title.
RA784.J65   1992
613.2—dc20   91–41867
                          CIP

Macmillan books are available at special discounts for bulk purchases for sales promotions, premiums, fund-raising, or educational use. For details, contact:

Special Sales Director
Macmillan Publishing Company
866 Third Avenue
New York, NY 10022

Book design by Maura Fadden Rosenthal

10   9   8   7   6   5   4   3   2   1

Printed in the United States of America

To Margret McBride, my literary agent and wonderful friend

Contents

I would like to thank the following people for their help on this book: Lynne W. Scott, M.A., R.D./L.D., for technical assistance; William Hansen; Bradley Chamberlin; Viola Stroup; Karma Kientzler; William Rosen; and my editor, Natalie Chapman, for perseverance above and beyond the call of duty.

Foreword

As a physician specializing in the prevention and treatment of heart disease, I have had a long interest in diet and the positive effect of a good diet on overall health. My particular specialty relates to how how what we eat can cause blood cholesterol to increase or decrease. One of the most common questions that patients ask me is "Will lowering blood cholesterol help prevent heart disease?" to which my answer is usually "Yes."

Results from laboratory, epidemiologic, and clinical studies show a very strong connection between diet, blood cholesterol level, and coronary heart disease. This relationship is based on the effect of saturated fatty acids, cholesterol, and obesity on blood cholesterol. A high level of blood cholesterol is one of the major risk factors for heart disease.

Diet also plays a significant role in controlling several of the other risk factors for heart disease—high blood pressure, obesity, and diabetes. High blood pressure can often be lowered by weight loss (if overweight) and by decreasing the intake of sodium. Both the amount and the type of food eaten are important in controlling diabetes.

Heart disease ranks number one as the cause of death in the United States. More than 6 million Americans have a history of heart attack or symptoms of the disease. About 1,500,000 people suffer a heart attack each year, and more than 500,000 of these are fatal.

Although heart disease does not usually manifest itself until the adult years, hardening of the arteries, which leads to heart disease, may begin in childhood and slowly progress into adulthood. Recently the National Cholesterol Education Program released guidelines for detecting and treating high blood cholesterol in children two years of age and older. I feel it is very important for families as a whole to develop good eating habits.

I have known Jeanne Jones for almost two decades, and during that time, I have been impressed with the practical information on food selection and cooking she has given to Americans through her books, lectures, newspaper columns, and magazine articles. *Eating Smart* brings a vast amount of valuable information about diet, nutrition, and good eating habits into a short, easily understood book. She brings a fresh and "doable" approach to eating smart. This is a book that will be of value to anyone who is concerned about a healthy diet.

Antonio M. Gotto, Jr., M.D., D.Phil.
Chairman of the Department of Medicine
Chief of Internal Medicine Service
Baylor College of Medicine and
The Methodist Hospital

Houston, Texas

Preface

A powerful link exists between diet and heart disease. An equally powerful link exists between diet and blood cholesterol levels. Research has shown that lowering high blood cholesterol can actually help prevent heart disease. The dietary components known to raise blood cholesterol levels are a high intake of saturated fatty acids and dietary cholesterol, along with excessive calories, which also lead to obesity.

In *Eating Smart*, Jeanne Jones gives easy-to-follow suggestions on how to reduce not only the total fat in your diet but also saturated fat, cholesterol, sodium, and total calories. Readers will find her practical advice on menu planning, shopping, and revising recipes to be especially useful.

Lynne W. Scott, M.A., R.D./L.D.

Introduction

This book is an outgrowth of twenty years' experience in
trying to forge an alliance between good health and good food.

At the time I first became deeply interested in good nutrition,
there wasn't anyone on the culinary scene between Adelle Davis
and James Beard. It was either bare-bones nutrition and brewer's
yeast or all of the butter and cream you could fit into the pan.

I didn't want to give up anything. I love food, I love everything
about it. I love to eat, I love to cook, and I love to entertain. I
also love to look good, feel good, and have lots of energy, and
I was convinced that the two could be combined. I decided that
my role and my career would be to take the middle of the road,
to combine nutrition with gastronomy—that is, to combine the
science of food with the art of food.

Because I learned to cook in the classic tradition at some of
the best and most prestigious cooking schools in the world, I
had the advantage of knowing how to make the originals of the
high-fat, high-calorie dishes. This knowledge served me well in

creating more healthful alternatives, or what my friends dubbed "low-fat fakes."

In 1970, I started a company called Kilo Kounters, a weight-loss program much like many of the popular programs available. After developing tasty low-fat recipes and planning healthful, low-calorie menus for Kilo Kounter classes for over a year, I realized that I had enough material for a book. Those recipes became the basis for my first cookbook, *The Calculating Cook*, published in 1972.

A few years later I started a menu consulting company and began designing menus for spas, including the Golden Door, Rancho La Puerta, and the Canyon Ranch. I developed recipes for medically oriented weight-loss programs such as the Pritikin Longevity Center in Santa Monica and the Scripps Clinic and Research Foundation in La Jolla. I also worked with restaurant and hotel chefs to revise some of their favorite recipes to be lower in calories, fat, cholesterol, and sodium.

Among the most challenging of these assignments was working with all the talented executive chefs of the Four Seasons Hotels to develop their alternative menu program. It was important to Issy Sharp, the founder and president of the company, not to lose the unique style of any of the chefs in the process of revising their dishes. So, after working with all of them as a group at the Four Seasons headquarters in Toronto, I traveled to each chef's hotel to meet with him individually on the recipes for his menus. The result is that each hotel's menu now includes several low-fat, low-calorie gourmet-quality selections. The program has been an enormous success and is acknowledged as a benchmark in the hotel industry.

After the publication of *The Calculating Cook* I went on to write twenty more books on cooking and entertaining. In 1985 I started a syndicated newspaper column called *Cook It Light,* which now reaches about thirty million people every week through King Features Syndicate. Since it is an interactive column, readers write and send their favorite recipes for me to revise so that they will be lower in calories, fat, cholesterol, and sodium without losing their original taste and texture. I also receive requests for basic nutrition information. So much nutritional hype and propaganda exist, designed to sell you food products you don't need, that it can be very confusing.

In addition, I frequently speak to Fortune 500 companies, insurance groups, and health organizations throughout the world. Good nutrition is my favorite lecture subject because the audience response is so positive and rewarding. My talks usually focus on the fundamentals of nutrition—the information people need to take good care of themselves. I try to stay with essentials and convey the key concepts rather than delve into dense complexities that interest few and complicate the subject for many. Invariably, after a lecture, audience members come up to me and say, "Finally, I really get it. You clarified so many things about nutrition that I've always found confusing." Or, "At last this all makes sense to me."

This book is an attempt to distill every lecture I've ever given and every recipe I have ever created or revised. This single basic primer is intended to cover the fundamentals you need to become "literate" in smart eating. It is my honest belief that you don't need a complicated, thousand-page tome on nutrition in order to take charge of your own well-being. What you need to know is which foods are the best for you and which foods are potentially detrimental to your health—in other words, what and how much to eat. I know you don't want to give up anything you love any more than I do. This book was born from my desire to share with you how you can have it all—glorious food and glowing health.

You Are What You Eat

This year you are going to spend at least one thousand hours eating. Awesome thought, isn't it? Especially when you realize that those hours of eating can be used to provide you with more energy, a better body, and probably a longer life, or they can be spent destroying your health, adding unwanted pounds, and possibly shortening your life.

Spending those thousand-plus hours eating in a positive and pleasurable way is not difficult. All it takes is a little basic knowledge of nutrition so that you can make the right choices. That's what this book is intended to do—to give you the ABCs of food literacy you need to help you eat well, feel healthy, and look good for the rest of your life. In other words, it's all about Eating Smart!

Let's start with an obvious but fundamental point.

The body you're born with must last a lifetime. Like a well-maintained machine, it requires proper care and top-quality fuel to stay in good working order. If it wears out, there are no easily

You are issued only one body at birth.

installed replacement parts; if you feed it the wrong fuel and cause damage, you can't simply install a new engine. Therefore, proper fuel and good maintenance are essential to high performance and long-term use.

Food Is Your Only Fuel

All you have to "run on" is what you put in your mouth. The quality of your fuel and, therefore, the quality of your performance depends totally on what you eat and drink. It is essential, then, to learn the best possible fueling strategy for the best and longest-lasting performance.

Limited Fuel sources—foods high in fat, cholesterol, salt, sugar, and alcohol—will make you fat, clog your arteries, and raise your blood pressure.

Preferred Fuel sources—foods low in fat, cholesterol, salt, sugar, and alcohol—will improve your looks, benefit your health, and improve your mind.

Let's look at each of these benefits separately.

* **Improve your looks:** You can look better by maintaining a slim body. Being overweight is unattractive and makes you look older. The quality of your skin and hair is also improved with Preferred Fuel.
* **Improve your health:** Your health is affected enormously by what you eat. A high-fat diet, especially one high in saturated fats, can increase your risk for cancer and other degenerative diseases such as heart disease.

✻ **Increase your stamina:** Eating Smart increases your energy level and provides you with the stamina to enjoy life more fully.

Take a moment to ask yourself some important questions:

Do you like the way you look?

Are you at your ideal weight?

How are you really feeling?

Are your cholesterol and blood pressure within safe limits?

How is your energy? Are you feeling like a slick racing machine or a rusted-out clunker?

You have a choice when fueling your body. You can treat it like the magnificent machine it can be, or you can use low-octane fuel that causes knocks and pings.

Just knowing which foods should be considered Preferred Fuel and which foods should be Limited Fuel is a great start. That knowledge alone will make it possible for you to enjoy eating *all* the foods you like best. You can eat some of them abundantly and others in moderation, you really can have your cake and eat it too—as long as you're not eating too much cake or eating it too often.

Most "dieters" are always on some deprivation program they call the "new diet." Then, when their willpower runs out, they gorge on everything they've been denying themselves. They're obsessed with food and weight, and the more obsessed they become, the fatter they get and the worse they feel.

A large percentage of the people in this country are twenty pounds or more overweight. That means millions of fat Americans. Most of them diet continually; others use diet drugs that are potentially dangerous. With these methods the results are almost always the same: a weight loss followed by a weight gain that is usually more than was lost in the first place. Your goal is to lose weight safely and keep it off, control your cholesterol, and provide maximum protection against disease.

This book offers a simple, easily understood explanation of

Knowledge of good nutrition can change your life.

all the basic nutrition information needed to change your life. It is a complete manual for a better body.

Basic nutrition is a simple subject. There are only three kinds of food, and there are only four sources of calories. The next chapter explains these three food groups or fuel sources and shows you where calories come from. You can start Eating Smart immediately.

Fuel
Sources

2

Whenever I give lectures on Eating Smart, whether it's for a Fortune 500 company or for guests at the Canyon Ranch Health Resorts, I hear the same questions: "How can eggs have fat in them? I was told they were pure protein." "The bread I buy says enriched. Doesn't that mean it has all the nutrients and fiber put back in it?" "Doesn't 'fat reduced' mean most of the fat has been taken out?"

It takes a certain amount of knowledge about nutrition to ask questions like these. In fact, the subject of nutrition has become so popular in recent years that there is now a huge amount of information out there—much of it valuable but too much of it unreliable. It's very easy to get confused. In this chapter I'll try to pare it all down to the essentials.

Almost everything we eat and drink provides calories in the form of one of the following:

1. ■ Carbohydrates
2. ■ Proteins
3. ■ Fats

Carbohydrates are our best source of energy because they burn faster and more efficiently than either protein or fat.

Proteins contain amino acids which are the body's building blocks. Protein-rich foods contain the essential minerals and amino acids needed for the growth, maintenance, and repair of body cells. Foods high in protein don't provide energy as quickly as carbohydrate-rich foods.

Fats are greasy solid and liquid substances found in foods from both plants and animals. Some fat is necessary for good health, since fats enable us to absorb vitamins that are not water-soluble (such as vitamins A and E). However, you don't need to eat fats to get fat. Your body manufactures fat from the protein- and carbohydrate-rich foods you eat whenever you consume more than you need. This fat is stored to be used for energy whenever carbohydrates are not available, but it does not offer the same quick energy as do carbohydrate-rich foods.

Carbohydrates

Carbohydrates are divided into two groups:

1. ■ Complex carbohydrates
2. ■ Simple carbohydrates

Complex Carbohydrates

Complex carbohydrates are often described as starches. They include all grain products and vegetables, such as breads, cereals, pastas, corn, rice, beets, carrots, tomatoes, and potatoes, and all leafy greens such as lettuce, cabbage, and spinach. Foods rich in complex carbohydrates contain protein and often some fat as well. They are excellent sources of vitamins, minerals, and fiber.

Simple Carbohydrates

Simple carbohydrates are often described as sugars. They include both refined sugars, such as cane, beet, and brown sugars, and syrups, such as honey, maple syrup, and molasses. Also included in this category are foods high in these concentrated sweets, such as candies, jams, jellies, and sweetened carbonated beverages. Naturally occurring simple carbohydrates include both fresh and dried fruits and fruit juices, such as banana, apricot, pineapple, apple, and orange. Also included in this category is milk, which is naturally high in lactose, or "milk sugar."

Sugars include any ingredient ending in "ose," such as:

sucrose (ordinary table sugar)	lactose
fructose	dextrose
glucose	maltose

DIETARY FIBER

Dietary fiber is found only in foods of plant origin. There are two types of dietary fiber, soluble and insoluble. Studies have shown that soluble fiber added to a diet low in saturated fat and cholesterol lowers blood cholesterol. Good sources of soluble fiber include oat bran, oatmeal, beans, barley, and pectin found in some fruits and vegetables.

Insoluble fiber, found in wheat bran, whole wheat breads and cereals, and vegetables and their skins and peels, provides protection against colon cancer and helps with bowel function. Most fiber-containing foods have a combination of both soluble and insoluble fiber.

In some people simple carbohydrates can cause a rapid rise in blood sugar level, giving an immediate burst of energy, followed by a rapid drop in blood sugar level that can cause a feeling

There is no fiber in any food of animal origin.

of hunger and weakness. This peak-and-valley effect is often referred to as sugar highs and lows.

Proteins

Foods high in protein are divided into two groups:

1. ■ Animal protein (such as fish, poultry, meat, dairy products, and eggs)
2. ■ Plant protein (such as legumes, whole grains, vegetables, and other complex carbohydrates)

Animal Protein

Animal protein is any protein of animal origin, and it includes the following:

Fish and shellfish (such as salmon, tuna, shrimp, and lobster)

Poultry (such as chicken, turkey, duck, and pheasant)

Meat (such as beef, pork, lamb, and venison)

Dairy products (such as milk, cream, cheese, and yogurt)

Eggs of all types

Fish is a good source of animal protein. Most fish is lower in fat than poultry or meat.

Poultry, when eaten without skin, is lower in fat than most meat.

Meat is divided into three grades—prime, choice, and select—that are determined by its marbling, which consists of streaks of fat running through the red muscle of the meat. Prime grade contains the most marbling, followed by choice, and then select, which contains the least amount of fat. Prime cuts of meat should be avoided, when possible.

Dairy products are categorized by the amount of butterfat they contain.

Milk is divided into three categories: nonfat or skim, low-fat (½ percent to 2 percent butterfat), and whole milk (at least 3½ percent butterfat).

Nonfat or skim milk has more calcium and vitamins per volume than is found in low-fat and whole milk because it does not have fat displacing the other nutrients. It is also lower in cholesterol and calories.

Foods rich in animal protein contain varying amounts of fat and cholesterol. There is no cholesterol in any food of plant origin.

When buying dairy products, look for reduced-fat content on labels, such as nonfat yogurt; nonfat or low-fat cottage cheese; nonfat, part-skim, or low-fat ricotta; or part-skim mozzarella. The terminology varies depending on the dairy laws of the state.

Egg whites are pure protein. Egg yolks contain both cholesterol and saturated fat. In fact, there are 213 milligrams of cholesterol in one egg yolk, which is more than two-thirds of the American Heart Association's recommended maximum of 300 milligrams of cholesterol per day.

Plant Protein

Plant protein is found in all unrefined plant foods.
Good sources of plant protein include the following:

Legumes (all dried beans and peas, such as kidney beans, black-eyed peas, and soybeans)

Products from legumes (tofu, or soybean curd; tempeh; unhomogenized or natural peanut butter)

Animal protein contains all nine of the essential amino acids the body does not manufacture and must get from food. These essential amino acids are also found in plants, but not all in the same plants. It is necessary, therefore, to combine plants that contain some of the amino acids with plants that contain the others. This is why legumes and grains complement each other so well. Together they provide the same usable protein found in animal foods. Good examples of this "combining" are beans and rice, black-eyed peas and cornbread, and peanut butter on whole wheat bread.

Unrefined plant proteins contain fiber and sometimes fat. They do not contain cholesterol.

FAT IN MILK

To illustrate the dramatic differences in the three categories of milk, imagine an 8-ounce glass of nonfat milk. To turn this nonfat milk into 2 percent low-fat milk, add one pat or one teaspoon of melted butter and stir until it is completely dissolved. To turn the low-fat milk you just made into whole milk, add still another pat or teaspoon of butter. Remember, the next time you want a glass of whole milk, you are actually reaching for a glass of nonfat milk and two pats of butter.

Skim  *2% Fat*  *Whole*

	Skim	*2% Fat*	*Whole*
Total Calories:	*87*	*123*	*152*
Percentage of Calories from Fat:	*5%*	*35%*	*49%*
Fat (grams):	*4 g*	*5 g*	*8 g*
Cholesterol (milligrams):	*5 mg*	*19 mg*	*34 mg*

12

Q & A

Question: *Does combining any grain and any legume give you a complete protein, or just certain ones?*

Answer: *Any grain (wheat, rice, corn, barley, and so forth) combined with any legume (kidney beans, black-eyed peas, peanuts, and so forth) constitutes a complete and usable protein.*

Nuts and seeds are also good sources of protein; however, they contain too much fat to be used as a regular source of vegetable protein. In fact, they are often classified as fats. Use them only occasionally for flavor and texture.

Other foods often classified as proteins that are high in fat include many cheeses, fat-marbled meat (such as bacon), and the skin of poultry.

Fats

Fats are divided into three groups:

1. ■ Saturated
2. ■ Polyunsaturated
3. ■ Monounsaturated

Many people do not realize that all fats are actually a mix of saturated, polyunsaturated, and monounsaturated fats. Since proportions vary greatly, however, fats are categorized by the predominant type of fatty acids they contain.

Saturated Fats

Fats of animal origin and coconut oil, palm kernel oil, palm oil, and cocoa butter are all predominantly saturated fats. They are solid or semisolid at room temperature (70°F). These are some of the sources:

> Poultry (all visible fat, the skin, and fat rendered from cooking poultry)
>
> Meat (all visible fat, including marbling or the veins of fat running through the lean muscle)
>
> Butter and butterfat (fat found in milk, cheese, cream, and ice cream)
>
> Eggs (fat found in egg yolks only)
>
> Coconut oil
>
> Palm kernel oil
>
> Palm oil
>
> Cocoa butter (fat found in chocolate)

Saturated fats are the least desirable of all the fats and should be limited or avoided whenever possible. They contribute to the buildup of both the cholesterol we make in our own bodies and the cholesterol derived from other sources.

Saturated fats of animal origin also contain cholesterol. Coconut oil and palm kernel oil do not because they are derived from plants; nevertheless, they should be avoided because they are "highly saturated" fats and elevate cholesterol.

Question: *Is it true that coconut contains lots of cholesterol?*

Answer: *No. Coconut is a plant, and cholesterol is found only in foods of animal origin. Coconut is a highly saturated fat, however, and should be avoided by anyone on a low-cholesterol diet. Saturated fat is the culprit in depositing cholesterol on artery walls.*

Polyunsaturated Fats

Fats that are primarily polyunsaturated are of plant origin. They are liquid at room temperature. The following are sources:

Safflower oil	Corn oil
Soybean oil	Cottonseed oil
Sunflower oil	

Polyunsaturated fats were once thought to aid in reducing the buildup of cholesterol in the blood vessels. Current research

WHAT IS
CHOLESTEROL?

Cholesterol is found in all foods of animal origin, and it is also produced by the body. A certain amount of it is necessary for good health. When too much of it is present in the body, however, it can build up on the interior artery walls, narrowing and roughening the vessels through which the blood flows, and cause heart disease.

There are two types of blood cholesterol: Low-density lipoprotein cholesterol, or LDL, is bad. High-density lipoprotein cholesterol, or HDL, is good.

LDL accelerates the buildup of cholesterol inside the blood vessels. Studies have shown that the higher the LDL level, the greater the risk of heart disease. A diet high in saturated fats and cholesterol-rich foods such as eggs, meats, organ meats, and many dairy products can increase the level of the potentially dangerous LDLs.

HDL, on the other hand, actually helps remove cholesterol from your bloodstream, reducing the risk of heart disease.

This doesn't mean you can never eat eggs or other high-cholesterol foods again, but it does mean you should limit them. In other words, if you have a two-egg omelet for breakfast, you certainly don't want to have liver for dinner.

16

indicates, however, that polyunsaturated fats reduce both the "good" (HDL) cholesterol along with the "bad" (LDL) cholesterol and therefore should be limited.

Monounsaturated Fats

Fats that are primarily monounsaturated are also of plant origin. They are liquid at room temperature. These are some sources:

Olive oil	Peanut oil
Canola oil	Avocado oil

Monounsaturated fats lower the "bad" (LDL) cholesterol without lowering the "good" (HDL) cholesterol. Whenever adding fat on purpose, try to choose a predominantly monounsaturated fat.

Q & A

Question: *Is there anything I can eat to raise my HDL cholesterol?*

Answer: *The goal is not to raise your HDL, but to lower your LDL and improve the ratio of HDL to LDL cholesterol. This is accomplished by lowering your intake of saturated fats and cholesterol-rich foods, and increasing your intake of dietary fiber.*

Hydrogenated Fats

Hydrogenated fats are predominantly polyunsaturated and monounsaturated fats that have been processed to turn them from liquids into semisolids. How solid they are depends on the extent of hydrogenation. Some sources are as follows:

Margarine

Solid vegetable shortening (such as Crisco)

Homogenized peanut butter

Hydrogenated fats tend to act like saturated fats in the body and therefore should be limited. Many products are labeled "partially hydrogenated"; while partially hydrogenated may be better than fully hydrogenated oil, that does not mean it is good for you!

When using margarine choose a "tub" rather than a stick, and make sure it is pure corn, or safflower, or sunflower oil margarine rather than a blend containing coconut or palm kernel oil. Use vegetable oils such as olive oil or canola oil rather than solid vegetable shortening. Always select unhomogenized or "old-fashioned" peanut butter rather than homogenized peanut butter.

Fuel Additives

Besides the three basic components of food (carbohydrates, proteins, and fats), there are also what might be called *fuel additives*. Sources include the following:

Water (bottled, fresh, carbonated, noncarbonated, and distilled)

Salt (table salt, monosodium glutamate [MSG], seasonings with a high-sodium content such as soy sauce and Worcestershire, and most preservatives)

Salt substitutes

Sugar substitutes (saccharin, aspartame, and cyclamates)

Caffeine (coffee, tea, chocolate, and cola beverages)

Seasonings of all types (herbs, herb blends, spices, extracts, and sauces such as Tabasco)

Most of these food additives are calorie-free, with the exception of chocolate and cola beverages. Items sometimes categorized as condiments, such as mustard and catsup, are better classified as foods.

WATER: The Wonder Drink

Six to eight glasses of plain water a day will improve your general health and help you to have beautiful, clear skin. Adequate water is necessary to dilute the impurities or waste materials eventually excreted by the body so that the kidneys aren't overworked. Water also acts as a natural diuretic. It's just like priming the pump—the more water you drink, the less you retain. Water also helps prevent overheating and dehydration.

It is essential for you to drink an adequate amount of water. If you drink an insufficient amount, the fiber or bulk will stop moving through your body after all available moisture has been absorbed. Many people think they can't eat high-fiber foods because doing so slows down their digestion. The problem is that they don't drink enough water to keep the fiber moving.

Coffee, tea, and diet drinks are not water substitutes! Six to eight glasses of water means just that—pure water. In fact, both coffee and alcohol speed up dehydration.

If you don't like the taste of your tap water or you live in an area where the water's sodium content is high, buy bottled water. If you are already on a sodium-restricted diet, it's best to drink distilled water, which contains no sodium.

Naturally occurring sparkling water such as Perrier, Poland Spring, and Calistoga waters are lower in sodium than regular soda water. So are salt-free seltzers, both flavored and unflavored. Any of these waters is acceptable in meeting your daily water requirement.

Using Less Salt Without Missing It

Reducing the amount of sodium added to the fuel mix is important for good health and essential for practicing good preventive medicine. Salt is sodium chloride. Salt is not a food and does not contain calories, but if you eat too much salt, fluid accumulates in your body, causing you to look and feel bloated. Many people falsely believe salt is fattening because the fluid retention increases their weight. If you wake up in the morning with puffy eyelids, your body may be trying to tell you that you have been consuming too much salt and drinking too little water.

Excessive sodium intake has been linked to many health problems, among them strokes, damage to the arteries, high blood pressure, and hypertension.

One level teaspoon of salt contains almost 2,000 milligrams of sodium. According to the American Heart Association, no one should consume more than 3,000 milligrams of sodium a day. Since sodium is present in varying degrees in everything except distilled water, always taste before adding salt. Foods high in sodium include most cheeses, pickles and olives, many condiments (such as mustard and catsup), canned soups and sauces, sauerkraut, and dry cereals.

Salt is not a seasoning. It was used as a preservative for so long that people acquired a taste for it. After you consciously reduce the amount of salt you use in cooking and avoid adding salt to your meals whenever possible, you will find that you almost immediately lose your taste for salty foods even if you were a salt addict who salted first, then tasted. Also, salt is not a drug like caffeine, and therefore giving it up causes no unpleasant side effects.

MSG, or monosodium glutamate, another fuel additive, is extremely high in sodium. It is often used to improve the taste of poor ingredients in commercially prepared foods and in restaurants and is frequently used in Oriental cooking. Many people suffer marked physical reactions such as headaches and a tingling sensation or hot flash after eating anything containing MSG. Other reactions include swollen ankles and feet.

Question: *Are there any salt substitutes "worth their salt"?*

Answer: *I do not recommend salt substitutes. Those made from potassium have a terrible metallic aftertaste when heated. Some substitutes also contain sodium and should be used sparingly. Learning to enjoy food without added salt and to use herbs and spices liberally is the best course.*

Sugar Substitutes Do Not Help Weight Loss

Many artificial sweeteners are not good substitutes for sugar because they contain chemicals the body doesn't need. Some are potentially dangerous, and they distort the perception of natural sweetness. Just watch a person who usually uses a sugar substitute in coffee as he or she uses real sugar when that's all that's available. The person will add a heaping teaspoonful of sugar, taste it, add another heaping teaspoonful, taste it, and then usually add still another in an attempt to bring the coffee to the accustomed level of sweetness obtained from the artificial sweetener.

The longer you use artificial sweeteners, the more you need. If you must, it's better to use a small amount of table sugar in your coffee; there are only 16 calories in a teaspoonful.

Foods high in artificial sweeteners include most so-called diet desserts and diet soft drinks. Ironically, none of the sugar substitutes has ever been conclusively shown to help weight loss.

Caffeine Is a Drug

The drug caffeine acts as a stimulant, giving you a false sense of energy. Since caffeine actually lowers blood sugar, you have less energy once the caffeine "high" has faded. You also feel hungry! If you continue this cycle of drinking more coffee or tea for more energy, you will get what is often called coffee nerves—a shaky, irritable feeling that is mood-altering.

Caffeine causes other side effects, such as sleeplessness, anxiety, and heartburn, and has been associated with the growth of fibrous cysts in women's breasts.

Decaffeinated coffee contains less than 6 milligrams of caffeine per 5-ounce cup, compared to regular coffee that has about 90 milligrams of caffeine in a 5-ounce cup.

Some coffee is decaffeinated by a chemical process that has been shown to cause cancer in laboratory animals. Make sure yours has been decaffeinated by the Swiss, or water-washed, method.

Vitamins and Minerals

Vitamins are complex chemicals that are essential for the normal functioning of the body. There are thirteen major vitamins: A, C, D, E, K, B_{12}, and the seven B-complex vitamins (thiamine, riboflavin, niacin, pantothenic acid, pyridoxine, biotin, and folic acid).

Most vitamins are required only in extremely small amounts, and each vitamin is found in many different foods. Vitamin D is also produced in the skin when it is exposed to sunlight.

A well-balanced diet that includes a variety of foods is likely to contain adequate amounts of all vitamins, and supplements are not usually necessary. For vegetarians who eat no animal products, vitamin B_{12} and D may be lacking. These vitamins can be obtained from supplements or, in the case of vitamin D, from adequate exposure to sunlight.

Vitamins are divided into two types: fat-soluble and water-soluble. *Fat-soluble vitamins* (A, D, E, and K) are absorbed with fats from the intestine into the blood and then stored in fatty tissue (mainly the liver). They are not normally excreted in the urine. An excessive intake of fat-soluble vitamins may cause harmful levels to accumulate in the body. For most people a balanced diet ensures a sufficient supply.

Water-soluble vitamins are C, B_{12}, and the B-complex vitamins. They are not stored in the body for long periods and are rapidly excreted in the urine if taken in greater amounts than the body requires. Vitamin B_{12} is an exception; it is stored in the liver.

You are more likely to be deficient in water-soluble than fat-

23

DO YOU NEED A VITAMIN OR MINERAL SUPPLEMENT?

If you are living in an area where fresh fruits and vegetables are not readily available and you must rely primarily on processed foods, which are not as rich in essential nutrients, many doctors and dietitians recommend taking a daily vitamin and mineral supplement. They consider it a nutritional insurance policy.

However, all nutrition experts warn against excessive consumption of a particular vitamin or mineral because you have read in a newspaper or magazine about the health benefits it offers. These benefits are derived from the minimum daily requirements of the vitamin or mineral, not from taking copious quantities.

Too much of any vitamin or mineral can cause your body to have a chemical imbalance. In fact, an overdose of some vitamins can be dangerous to your health. Remember, eating a variety of foods and maintaining a desirable weight is the goal.

soluble vitamins, so foods rich in water-soluble vitamins should be eaten daily. Also, prolonged cooking, preserving, and processing all tend to destroy these vitamins, so fresh or lightly cooked foods are the best sources.

Minerals are chemical elements that must be present in the diet for good health. Among the more important minerals are calcium, potassium, sodium, magnesium, and phosphorus.

Trace elements, a group of minerals vital to numerous chemical processes in the body, are required only in minute amounts. The most important are iron, chromium, copper, selenium, sulfur, and zinc. A well-balanced diet usually contains all the minerals, including trace elements, your body needs.

Nutrition in a Nutshell

Understanding where all foods come from and how they are used by your body is a great start to what I refer to as "nutrition in a nutshell." The next chapter completes the ABCs of food literacy by discussing how calories relate to all the fuel sources.

VITAMINS AND THEIR SOURCES IN THE DIET

Fat-soluble	Good sources
Vitamin A	Liver, fish-liver oils, egg yolk, milk and dairy products, margarine, yellow and orange fruits and vegetables (such as carrots and apricots)
Vitamin D	Fortified milk, oily fish (such as sardines, salmon, and tuna), liver, dairy products, egg yolk
Vitamin E	Vegetable oils (such as corn, soybean, olive, and sunflower oils), nuts, meat, green leafy vegetables, cereals, wheat germ, egg yolk
Vitamin K	Green leafy vegetables (especially cabbage, broccoli, and turnip greens), vegetable oils, egg yolk, cheese, pork, liver
Water-soluble	
Thiamine (vitamin B_1)	Wheat germ, bran, whole-grain or enriched cereals and breads, brown rice, pasta, liver, kidney, pork, fish, beans, nuts
Riboflavin (vitamin B_2)	Liver, milk, cheese, eggs, green leafy vegetables, whole grains, enriched breads and cereals, brewer's yeast
Niacin (nicotinic acid)	Liver, lean meat, poultry, fish, whole grains, enriched breads and cereals, peanuts, dried beans
Pantothenic acid	Liver, heart, kidney, fish, egg yolk, skim milk, brewer's yeast, wheat germ, most vegetables
Pyridoxine (vitamin B_6)	Liver, chicken, pork, fish, whole grains, wheat germ, bananas, potatoes, dried beans, peanuts
Biotin	Liver, kidney, peanuts, dried beans, egg yolk, mushrooms, cauliflower, bananas, grapefruit, watermelons
Folic acid	Green leafy vegetables (such as spinach and broccoli), mushrooms, liver, nuts, dried beans, peas, egg yolk, whole wheat bread
Vitamin B_{12} (cyanocobalamin)	Liver, kidney, chicken, beef, pork, fish, eggs, cheese, butter, yogurt, other dairy products
Vitamin C	Citrus fruits, tomatoes, potatoes, green leafy vegetables, strawberries, cantaloupe

MINERALS AND MAIN FOOD SOURCES

Mineral	Sources
Calcium	Milk, cheese, butter and margarine, green vegetables, legumes, nuts, soybean products, hard water
Chromium	Red meat, cheese, butter and margarine, whole-grain cereals and breads, green vegetables
Copper	Red meat, poultry, liver, fish, seafood, whole-grain cereals and breads, green vegetables, legumes, nuts, raisins, mushrooms
Fluorine	Fish, fluoridated water, tea
Iodine	Milk, cheese, butter and margarine, fish, whole-grain cereals and breads, iodized table salt
Iron	Red meat, poultry, liver, eggs, fish, whole-grain cereals and breads
Magnesium	Milk, fish, whole-grain cereals and breads, green vegetables, legumes, nuts, hard water
Phosphorus	Red meat, poultry, liver, milk, cheese, butter and margarine, eggs, fish, whole-grain cereals and breads, green vegetables, root vegetables, legumes, nuts, fruit
Potassium	Whole grain cereals and breads, green vegetables, legumes, fruit
Selenium	Red meat, liver, milk, fish, seafood, whole-grain cereals and breads
Sodium	Red meat, poultry, liver, milk, cheese, butter and margarine, eggs, fish, whole-grain cereals and breads, green vegetables, root vegetables, legumes, nuts, fruit, table salt, processed foods
Zinc	Red meat, fish, seafood, eggs, milk, whole-grain cereals and breads, legumes

Not All Calories Are Alike

3

ecently I was the keynote speaker for the opening of the Peninsula Spa, a state-of-the-art urban fitness club at the top of the Peninsula Hotel in New York City. For the occasion the hotel's executive chef created a wondrously delicious and stunningly beautiful brunch entree: a tall, cone-shaped tower of vanilla yogurt mousse resting on a crunchy granola cake in the middle of a swirling sea of colorful fruit purees.

The first question asked by one of the guests was "How many calories are in that granola cake?" My answer was "Who cares?"

The important thing to know about any meal is not how many calories or how much fat is in any one item but the total calories and how many of them come from fat.

Calories come from only four sources: the three food groups and alcohol.

The number of calories in one gram varies considerably depending on its source:

1. ■ Carbohydrates (both simple and complex): 4 calories per gram
2. ■ Proteins (both animal and plant): 4 calories per gram
3. ■ Fats (saturated, polyunsaturated, and monounsaturated): 9 calories per gram
4. ■ Alcohol (wine, beer, and distilled spirits): 7 calories per gram

Understanding Calorie Density

As you can see, fats have more than twice as many calories per gram as either carbohydrates or protein; therefore, fats have the greatest calorie density.

Many people have the wrong idea about how to lose weight. They think to lower calorie intake is to cut down on carbohydrate foods such as breads, cereals, potatoes, and pastas, and eat more protein foods such as poultry, meat, eggs, and cheese.

As I explained in the preceding chapter, a large percentage of animal protein is fat, not protein. Since fat has more than twice as many calories as protein, these people are actually adding calories instead of cutting them.

Picture yourself sitting at a table with an 8-ounce steak, an 8-ounce baked potato, and 8 ounces of steamed broccoli on a plate in front of you. If you chopped them all up and put them in measuring cups, you would have one cup of steak, two cups of potato, and three cups of broccoli.

Even though in terms of volume the steak is the smallest-sized portion on the plate, it has four times as many calories as the baked potato and twelve times as many calories as the steamed broccoli!

You can certainly see that if you are trying to cut calories, the first thing to do is cut the steak in half, not the potato and certainly not the broccoli.

It's not the protein in the steak that makes it so high in calories, it's the fat hiding in the red muscle, or the *calorie density*.

In general, vegetables offer the lowest calorie density of all food groups. Fruits have a higher calorie density than most vegetables. One piece of fruit with each meal and one as a snack is a recommended daily guideline. Dried fruits such as raisins, dates, prunes, and apricots have a higher calorie density than fresh fruits because they are dehydrated. They are handy for snacks, however, because they can be carried with you so easily.

Potatoes are not fattening. If you pile on the butter, margarine, sour cream, and chopped bacon, potatoes then become fattening because these additions are *fats*. Fortunately, you can leave the fat off a baked potato, but you can't get the fat out of a well-marbled steak.

In fact, potatoes get a bum rap all around. If people aren't piling fat on baked potatoes, they're mashing or scalloping them with butter and cream, deep-frying them until they're dripping with grease, or turning them into a salad loaded with mayonnaise. Then they end up calling the poor potato "fattening."

Here are some good examples of dramatic calorie increases when fat is added:

* Two pats of butter spread on a dinner roll have more calories than the roll itself. (Two tablespoons of butter or any fat has approximately 240 calories; the average dinner roll has 100.)
* A few tablespoons of the average salad dressing has more calories than the salad it's poured over. (Most salad dressings are about 100 calories per tablespoon; the average dinner salad is less than 50 calories.)
* Croissants and brioche rolls are made with equal amounts of butter and flour. That means more than two-thirds of the calories are coming from fat.

✳ Butter or margarine, sour cream, and chopped bacon added to a plain 8-ounce baked potato can increase the calories from 240 to over 1,000.

Alcohol: Double Trouble When You're Eating Smart

Although not classified as a food, alcohol does contain calories— a whopping 7 calories per gram. Alcohol can give you an overload of calories without any other nutritional benefit, so one or two drinks a day is the maximum for high-performance people. You need the rest of your calories to provide your body with necessary vitamins, minerals, and fiber.

What is a drink? A drink is a jigger, one and a half ounces, of distilled spirits or hard liquor. It is also equivalent to two 12-ounce glasses of beer or two 5-ounce glasses of wine.

The calorie density of alcoholic beverages can be lessened by adding more water or soda water to mixed drinks, by drinking "lite" beer, and by mixing wine with soda water for wine spritzers. Avoid liqueurs and sweet cocktails.

The "double trouble" of alcohol is that it lowers your blood sugar, causing you to become hungry, and at the same time goes directly to the judgment center of your brain, lowering your willpower. This combination of increased appetite and decreased willpower will cause you to eat junk foods that you normally wouldn't eat and to take in more fuel than you need.

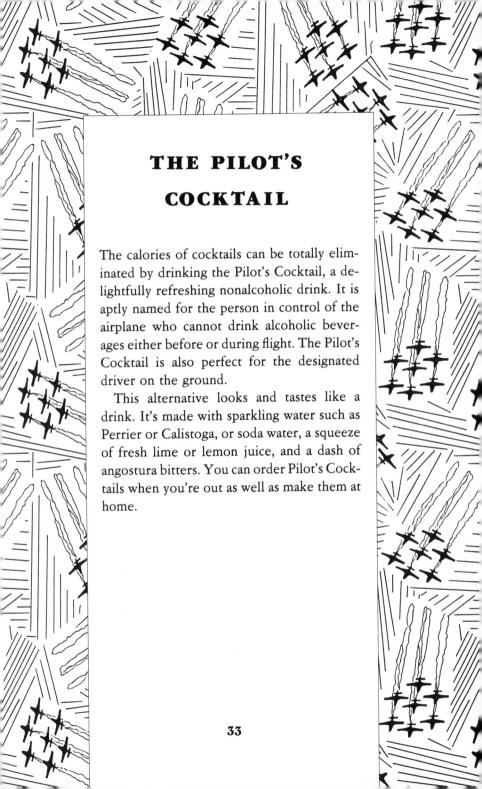

THE PILOT'S
COCKTAIL

The calories of cocktails can be totally eliminated by drinking the Pilot's Cocktail, a delightfully refreshing nonalcoholic drink. It is aptly named for the person in control of the airplane who cannot drink alcoholic beverages either before or during flight. The Pilot's Cocktail is also perfect for the designated driver on the ground.

This alternative looks and tastes like a drink. It's made with sparkling water such as Perrier or Calistoga, or soda water, a squeeze of fresh lime or lemon juice, and a dash of angostura bitters. You can order Pilot's Cocktails when you're out as well as make them at home.

Q & A

Question: *Is beer more nutritious than wine or hard liquor?*

Answer: *One 12-ounce can of beer contains more calories and is slightly more nutritious than a 5-ounce glass of wine or a jigger of hard liquor. The beer and wine both contain vitamins and minerals, and carbohydrates, so they are not completely "empty" calories. Other than alcohol and taste, there is little to redeem hard liquor.*

When drinking wine with a meal, always have a glass of water as well. Drinking the water alternately with the wine will help reduce the amount of wine you drink. In this way you don't have to give up the enjoyment of wine with your meal or wake up regretting it the next morning.

Limiting Fat Calories

At this point you might be asking yourself, "Why be so concerned about the percentage of calories from fat?"

Too much fat is hazardous to your health.

Just how drastically should you limit your fat intake? Opinion varies.

The American Heart Association tells us that we should not be consuming more than 30 percent of our calories from fat each day.

The Pritikin program was founded on the concept that we should not be consuming more than 10 percent of our calories from fat each day.

The average American diet contains nearly 40 percent fat!

Exactly what does 30 percent or 10 percent total calories coming from fat each day mean in terms of what we eat?

Let me give you an example of how difficult a concept this is for many people to grasp. When I was designing the menus for the Pritikin Longevity Center in California, I served as a counselor on a two-week Pritikin cruise through the Panama Canal. All of the more than one hundred participants had just completed the twenty-six-day program at the center.

The second day out, I was shocked to see a group of participants eating ice cream cones. When I asked them why they were off their diets, they told me, "We're just eating the 10 percent fat we're allowed today in ice cream." They really believed that the amount of ice cream they were eating was so small in comparison with the amount of high-fiber, low-fat, and nonfat foods in the rest of their daily diet that the ice cream was "legal."

Here is what these dieters were doing:

Their total calories for the day	2,000
Fat calories allowed for the day (10 percent of total)	200
Total grams of fat in one ice cream cone	27
Total calories from fat in one ice cream cone (9 calories per gram of fat times 27 grams of fat)	243

These people had used up—indeed, exceeded—their entire daily quota of fat calories in a single snack. Even if nothing else they ate that day had a single gram of fat, they would already have blown their diets.

But there's some fat in almost everything we eat. In a breakfast of a half grapefruit, a slice of whole wheat toast, and an 8-ounce glass of low-fat milk, you'll get 1 gram of fat in the unbuttered toast and 4 grams of fat in the milk. In a lunch of water-packed tuna salad with two tablespoons of light mayonnaise dressing, you'll get 1 gram of fat from the tuna and 10 grams from the light mayonnaise. In a lean dinner of skinless grilled breast of chicken, green beans, and a half cup of rice pilaf, you'll get 2 grams of fat from the chicken, a trace from the beans, and 2 grams from the rice pilaf. Although that's about as lean a cuisine as you can find in a normal diet, note how many grams of fat you're eating even when you cut oil, butter, and sweets to an absolute minimum.

What my ice-cream-cone-eating friends did not understand and I hastened to explain at the next morning's lecture was that to keep your calories from fat as low as 10 percent of the total calories you consume means that you can't add *any* fat to anything you eat. Keeping your fat intake under 10 percent of the total calories consumed is extremely difficult to accomplish as well as to understand.

You can do it if you're willing to read product labels, do an easy, in-your-head computation (see sidebar), and monitor everything you eat.

But you want to be able to eat in restaurants, entertain at home, and travel without constantly worrying about what you are eating. And perhaps you wonder whether a 10 percent ceiling on fat calories is too low, especially considering the conflicting advice of different experts and programs. No matter what percentage of fat is advised—10 percent or 30 percent—the essential message of all health and nutrition experts is the same: *fight fat.*

36

To make that goal easier to accomplish, let's do two things.

First, let's take a "middle of the road" approach between the 10 percent fat school and the 30 percent fat advocates. Let's say that 20 percent of the calories you consume each day can come from fat. In fact, this number is probably "safer" than aiming for 30 percent because it gives you a built-in margin for error.

Second, let's focus less on numbers and computations and more on the main point: reducing the proportion of fat in your diet to no more than 20 percent. The simple way to do that is to follow the Five-to-One Formula, which I'll tell you about in the next chapter.

HOW TO COMPUTE
THE PERCENTAGE OF
CALORIES FROM FAT

To make it simpler, instead of computing fat calories at 9 calories per gram, let's round up to 10. (Ten calories per gram may in fact be more accurate. New research indicates that some fats may actually have between 10 and 12 calories per gram instead of 9.) To figure what percentage of your daily calories comes from fat, here's what you do:

1. ■ Read the label of a product to find out how many calories and how many grams of fat the product has per serving.

   Example: A can of chicken soup lists 100 calories and 4 grams of fat per serving.

2. ■ Multiply the number of grams of fat by 10. The result is the approximate number of fat calories per serving.

Example: 4 grams of fat × 10 = 40 fat calories per serving.

3. ■ To calculate the percentage of fat in that serving, divide the total number of calories into the number of fat calories.

$$\text{Example:} \frac{40 \text{ fat calories}}{100 \text{ total calories}} = .40 \text{ or } 40 \text{ percent}$$

If the label in the sample had listed 200 calories per serving, then the 40 calories from fat would be only 20 percent of its calories from fat (40 ÷ 200 = .20 or 20 percent).

Eating Smart Magic: The Five-to-One Formula

4

The Key to Success

Just knowing about the basic food groups, understanding their calorie densities, and being aware of fat content is a good start toward Eating Smart. The key to success, however, lies in how you apply your new food literacy. To make it easy, remember this basic formula:

Following the Five-to-One Formula automatically keeps you on a high-fiber, low-cholesterol, low-fat diet. It limits your fat intake to about 20 percent of the total calories consumed so that you never have to worry about the issue again.

You can break the habit (if you ever had it) of getting out your calorie counter or your fat finder chart every time you're about to eat anything. You can stop treating yourself like a

> *Eat five times as much carbohydrate foods as animal protein, and limit fat.*

laboratory animal who is allowed only a specific amount of certain nutrients at specific times of the day or night. You can start enjoying glorious food and growing healthy at the same time.

Old-fashioned, traditional menu planning always started with the question, "What will I serve with the roast?" The Five-to-One Formula for menu planning turns the question around. Think of fish, poultry, or meat as the side dish and the salad, vegetable, breads, and pastas as the main part of the meal.

Another way to visualize this is to picture six coffee cups lined up on your table. Think of filling five of them with your salad, vegetables, potatoes, rice, pasta or bread, and fruit. Now picture your fish, poultry, meat, cheese, or eggs in the coffee cup that is still empty. The cup doesn't have to be full. Animal protein doesn't need to constitute one-fifth of the volume of your meal; it simply should never be more than one-fifth of your meal.

This five-to-one "golden food rule" will indeed make every one of the thousand hours you spend eating each year a happier as well as a healthier occasion.

The beauty of the Five-to-One Formula is that you don't have to give up the foods you enjoy most. You simply learn to use common sense and moderation in selecting foods for your daily diet. You want to have a better body, better mind, and better life. Moderation is not martyrdom; you don't want to be deprived. The Five-to-One Formula offers maximum flexibility because you can eat anything as long as you combine the things you like best in the right ratio. It offers you a wide variety of tastes and textures that will make your meals more fun to prepare and more interesting to eat.

After using this formula for just a short time, your basic tastes will change. When you use less dressing on your salad, you'll undoubtedly start enjoying the fresh tastes and delightful crunchiness of fresh fruits and vegetables more than you ever have before. A salad swimming in dressing will no longer appeal to you; in fact, it will taste greasy!

Whole-grain and enriched breads offer such wonderful variety in taste and texture. Also, using less butter or margarine on your toast will give you a new appreciation of the wonderful textures you've been missing and will make overly buttered toast seem soggy.

The only time it's actually necessary to give up certain foods completely is when you decide to lose weight; then you must take in less fuel than you are burning. The extra fuel needed by the body will then come from stored fuel or body fat.

THE FIVE-TO-ONE FORMULA

Eat Five Times as Much Carbohydrate Foods as Animal Protein

CARBOHYDRATE FOODS	ANIMAL PROTEIN FOODS
Vegetables *Fruits*	*Fish*
Whole-grain products:	*Poultry*
Breads *Pasta*	*Lean meat*
Cereals	*Dairy products*

43

Trading Off

The occasional junk-food freak-out never killed anyone or made anyone fat. It's the total food strategy and life-style that's important. By trading off you'll never have to give up eating the foods you like best. Here are some helpful tips:

1. ■ If you have butter or margarine on your toast for breakfast, use less salad dressing on your salad at lunch.
2. ■ If you want Roquefort cheese on your salad at lunch, use just enough for flavor but not enough to camouflage the taste of the other wonderful ingredients in the salad. And have fresh fruit for dessert, not cheesecake!
3. ■ If you enjoy wine with your dinner, have a nonalcoholic Pilot's Cocktail (page 33) before dinner. If you prefer to have an alcoholic drink before dinner, then forgo the wine with the meal.
4. ■ If you want real sour cream on your baked potato, order broiled fish or poultry without skin and not a New York steak.
5. ■ If you're having a Big Mac attack, don't order a chocolate malt to go with it. Lemonade is a better choice.
6. ■ If you can't sit through a movie without a snack, buy unbuttered popcorn, not nachos.
7. ■ If you love Italian sausage on your pizza, order it and eat a slice or two, not the whole pizza.

Following the Five-to-One Formula does not mean that you can eat copious quantities of food as long as you are combining them in the right ratio. In other words, it's not okay to eat a 12-ounce steak as long as you balance it with five times as much in volume of vegetables, grains, and fruit.

Think instead in terms of a 3-ounce or 4-ounce steak, the size of an average quarter-pound hamburger, or a piece of chicken instead of half a chicken. Visualize the rest of your meal in proportion to your serving of animal protein. Imagine how much money you can save when your 8-ounce steak can be cut in half to serve two. Even better, the average whole chicken breast, boned, skinned, and halved, will yield two 3-ounce to 4-ounce cooked portions. What could be easier and less expensive?

How Much Fuel Is Enough?

It's not necessary to add any fat in a well-balanced eating program. Enough fat is available in animal protein and complex carbohydrate foods without adding any extra fat.

If you know that the fuel tank in your car holds only twenty gallons, would you put twenty-five gallons in it? Of course not! It would spill out and be potentially dangerous. It is equally dangerous to constantly overfuel your body.

If you need only a few hundred calories at a meal for energy, why put in a thousand? It won't spill out, but it certainly will bulge out. The average woman needs about 2,000 calories per day, and the average man about 2,500. This means that most women should get no more than 400 of their total calories from fat, and most men no more than 500. When you follow the Five-to-One Formula and stop eating when you're no longer hungry,

BASICS OF
EATING SMART

1. ■ At every meal eat at least five times as much carbohydrate foods as animal protein.
2. ■ Limit fat to no more than 20 percent of daily calories.
3. ■ Use sugar and salt sparingly.
4. ■ Drink six to eight glasses of water per day.
5. ■ Limit alcohol.
6. ■ Stop eating when you are no longer hungry.

these numbers will take care of themselves and you needn't worry about counting.

When you take in more fuel of any type than your body can use, it is stored as fat, which is potentially dangerous to your health and certainly detrimental to your appearance.

The fat that is most dangerous to your health is often the fat you can't see, the hidden fat that builds up inside your blood vessels and around your organs.

The visible fat that builds up on your stomach, hips, thighs, and even around your neck makes you look older and less attractive. It makes it more difficult to move around.

Skipping Meals

Sometimes we might be tempted to skip a meal to help limit our intake of calories and keep our weight under control; however, skipping any meal prevents effective weight management. Each time you eat, your metabolism is raised and you burn up the calories faster than if your stomach is empty. That's because when you skip a meal your body thinks it's starving and slows down metabolism. Therefore, it's better to have three smaller meals and a snack if necessary than one or two larger meals. Your metabolism will hum along at a higher rate, more efficiently burning up the calories you're taking in.

Skipping breakfast can be dangerous. Statistics show that an enormous number of Americans—35 percent to 45 percent—routinely skip the most important meal of the day. Just as its name indicates, with breakfast you are breaking the fast of the night, and you need the early-morning nourishment to produce

> *Fat is an accessory. If you eat it, you wear it!*

47

enough energy to keep you going through the morning. Numerous studies demonstrate that workers who skip breakfast become less efficient in the late morning hours, as do students, who have trouble concentrating on their studies.

The Winning Combination

Practically everyone who has ever been on a diet knows the feeling of wishing for a magic wand that could remove those extra pounds with a single wave. The insatiable desire for fast, easy weight loss is at the root of the constant stream of new diet books that flood bookstores each year. As we've all been told more times than we care to count, there really is no gimmick that will make dieting quick and easy. But there is one thing that helps considerably—so much so that it's almost tantamount to magic in the effect it has. That is exercise.

Exercise works in tandem with diet in several ways. Getting adequate exercise helps you control your appetite. It raises your metabolism so that you burn unwanted fat more rapidly. And your metabolism remains elevated for many hours after a workout, continuing to burn up calories faster.

If you get adequate exercise and follow the Five-to-One Formula when you eat, you're on a winning course.

Winning with Exercise

5

B alancing your diet with exercise is the key to a successful fitness program and the key to a healthier, happier you.

Exercise not only improves the way you look by burning off the calories you ingest, but it also improves the way you feel. By enhancing your circulation—pumping more oxygen into your brain—exercise also stimulates your intellect, your self-awareness, and your productivity. Companies all over the world are offering fitness programs for their employees because studies show that forty-five minutes of exercise a day can increase a person's productivity by hours. You have more energy, tire less easily, and feel more mentally alert, more physically fit, and therefore more capable of dealing with the tasks and problems that confront you.

Ultimately, a good fitness program will increase your self-respect, your self-confidence, and the respect of others for you because you stand taller, walk better, look radiant, and think more clearly. Add it all together, and it's fitness for a better body, mind, and spirit.

I call my early-morning aerobics class my "attitude adjustment" period. When I miss my six o'clock workout, my "sunny" disposition starts to deteriorate by midafternoon.

Many people ask me how I can get up so early every morning and go to an exercise class. The answer is, I don't think about it—nor do I get "dressed up" for it. I get out of bed, splash water on my face, put on a leotard and aerobic shoes, and drive to class.

At seven o'clock, when the class is over, I leave feeling awake and energized. I drive home, shower, and dress for the day, and by nine o'clock I have forgotten all about having gone to the exercise class in the first place.

Please understand, I am decidedly not a "morning person." I don't like to get up early and think or talk. But I've found that getting exercise over with while I'm still in the waking-up process is a wonderful way to work it into my life.

Whatever your personal fitness program, keep it light and fun, something you will look forward to doing every day. Accompany your stretching, breathing, and relaxing exercises with the music you like best—whether disco or Debussy. The beat of the music will also help you establish a rhythm for your breathing and movements. And for your cardiovascular exercises, pick the activity you enjoy most—walking, jogging, swimming, tennis, aerobic dancing, or even skipping rope.

Choosing the right time for your daily exercise routine depends on your schedule. Before breakfast is one of the best times because you will feel more stimulated throughout the day. Or do your exercises on your lunch hour or before going to bed. If you are tired and have to go out in the evening, a few simple exercises, some stretches, and a shower will restore you so that you think you just took a long nap. In fact, it's more beneficial for you than the nap.

An exercise program must be comprehensive to be effective. To be fit you need to develop strength, endurance, and flexibility.

Aerobic Fitness

Aerobic or cardiovascular exercises develop both strength and endurance. They strengthen the heart, enabling it to force the blood through the body slowly and steadily rather than in rapid, short pulsations that will wear it out. These exercises—swimming, bicycling, jumping rope, aerobic dancing, jogging, walking briskly—all require exertion. Your heart beats faster, and you begin to breathe more deeply. The blood vessels expand, carrying blood and oxygen to your working muscles. When your body takes in more than the ordinary amount of oxygen, you are burning calories more rapidly than normal. This continuous movement enables you to tone muscles and burn off fat at the same time.

Most skiers start working to get their leg muscles stronger and back in shape before skiing season. Dancers spend hours at the barre to strengthen their bodies so that their muscles are strong enough to dance gracefully. But we often overlook the fact that the heart muscle must work all the time and, therefore, it requires regular exercise to keep it performing efficiently. When the heart is stronger, it can do the same work with fewer beats per minute and is capable of greater peak exertion.

Aerobic fitness also means that your lungs are working closer to their full capacity, making more oxygen available for all your cells. Better oxygenation gives you more endurance, helps you think more clearly, and increases your enthusiasm for life.

Aerobic exercise also increases the number of capillaries, the smallest blood vessels in the body. New branches grow out into the arms, legs, and other parts, making more blood available to the muscles and organs so they can work better.

Aerobic exercise helps burn up the fats in the bloodstream that may precipitate hardening of the arteries. Weight-bearing exercise is also one of the best preventive measures for osteoporosis.

It is dangerous to start an aerobic exercise program without first having a complete physical examination so that you know exactly how to pace yourself. If you have not been getting regular or adequate aerobic exercise to keep your heart in good condition, then you must start slowly. You don't start teaching people how to dive by having them go onto a high diving board, and you can't start an aerobic program by running a marathon. Instead, slowly increase both the intensity and the duration of the exercise until you are sustaining an elevated heart rate for at least twenty minutes.

You should warm up slowly before any cardiovascular exercise

Question: *How long after a meal should you wait before exercising, and why?*

Answer: *Twenty to thirty minutes is long enough for most people to wait after a meal before starting an exercise regimen. However, if you have had a particularly large or heavy meal, you may find you will be more comfortable if you wait a little longer. Digestion requires an increase in blood and oxygen to the digestive organs, which means that exercising too soon after eating could deprive the muscles you are working of needed nutrients (blood and oxygen).*

or active sport, and you should always "walk it down"—bring down your level of exertion slowly rather than come to an abrupt halt.

Stretching for Flexibility

You can become very strong and develop great endurance through aerobics and still not be flexible. Flexibility requires regular stretching exercises.

Stretching is the most important component in exercise because as we become older our muscles become shorter and tauter, and we lose our flexibility range if we don't keep them "stretched out." Without stretching we are more susceptible to knee, hip, shoulder, and elbow injuries.

Flexibility also contributes more to your body language than either strength or endurance. When you watch someone walking at a distance, you can usually guess the person's age by the way he or she moves. Sometimes, however, we are surprised to find that a person we judged from a distance to be hardly more than a teenager is, in fact, an agile senior citizen.

Karma Kientzler, who was the fitness director for the Canyon Ranch Health Resort in Tucson for many years, says the best stretching teachers in the world are the animals. Watch cats and learn from them, she advises: They stretch all day as part of normal, instinctive movement. When lying down they seldom get up and start moving without first stretching, and neither should we.

There are many ways you may stretch throughout the day in the course of your normal activities. You can stretch in your automobile, aligning your spine against the car seat and readjusting your mirrors so that you have to sit tall to see out of them. You can stretch at your desk: Push your arms out straight against your desk and drop your head down between your arms.

FOUR

BASIC

STRETCHING

EXERCISES

Overhead Stretch

1. ■ Start in a standing position with feet shoulder-width apart and arms raised overhead. Be sure palms face in, pelvis is tucked under, and abdominal muscles are contracted.
2. ■ Reach your right arm up, exhaling. Relax arm and inhale.
3. ■ Reach your left arm up, exhaling. Relax arm and inhale.
4. ■ Repeat alternately five to ten times on each side, exhaling as you reach up, inhaling as you relax your arms.
5. ■ Shake out arms.

Side Stretch

1. ■ Start in a standing position with feet shoulder-width apart and arms outstretched, palms down.
2. ■ Without moving your hips, move your torso and reach to the right, exhaling as you do so.
3. ■ Inhaling, return to the starting position.
4. ■ Exhaling, reach left. Then, inhaling, return to the starting position.
5. ■ Repeat alternately seven times on each side, exhaling as you reach, inhaling as you relax.
6. ■ Shake out arms.

Leg Stretch

1. ■ Start in a standing position with feet slightly apart, hands on your hips, and a tall spine. Inhale.
2. ■ Move your right leg forward and, exhaling, slowly bend your right knee, keeping feet straight forward and heels down. Slowly move your pelvis forward until your knee obscures your foot.
3. ■ Hold this stretch for five to ten seconds, breathing evenly.
4. ■ Repeat four times on each side.
5. ■ Shake out.

Sit-and-Reach Stretch

1. ■ Start in a sitting position with legs extended and hands on your knees. Inhale.
2. ■ Exhaling slowly, slide your hands down your legs as far as you can reach comfortably. Tuck in your chin, round your back, and contract your abdominal muscles. Reach for your ankles and hold for five seconds, breathing evenly.
3. ■ Inhaling, slowly return to the starting position.
4. ■ Repeat eight to ten times.

You can stretch when you reach down to a bottom drawer or up to a top shelf. You can stretch when you open a door: Instead of walking right up to the door handle, stop a little way off, flex your knees, and reach out. Whether you're standing or sitting, a few head and shoulder rolls feel wonderful anytime.

Stretching classes, ballet, yoga, t'ai chi ch'uan, and swimming are all excellent for improving flexibilty.

You can also greatly improve your flexibility with just a few basic stretches each day (see sidebar). While doing your stretching exercises, go slowly and gently at first. Do not strain your muscles beyond what you can do comfortably. If at first you can't touch your toes, don't worry. Reach as far as you can go or bend your knees slightly. Later, as your muscles become more flexible, you will do these things easily.

Some days you will be more flexible than others, which is perfectly normal. Once you are in a comfortable stretch, hold it for thirty seconds and don't forget to breathe while you're holding the stretch. In fact, try to stretch a little farther on each exhalation. Don't bounce. As you become more flexible, you can hold each stretch a little longer. You will be amazed how quickly your range of flexibility increases.

Small Changes Can Make a Big Difference

Dr. Kenneth Cooper, often called the father of aerobics, says, "It doesn't take that much exercise to see some tremendous benefits." And in fact you can build exercise into your current life-style with very little alteration.

Walking

Walking is a most rewarding exercise and is good for everyone. We've all been told that jogging is excellent exercise, but in fact more and more joggers are becoming walkers because of the injuries and damage running can cause. Walking is easier on you yet still lets you exercise your whole body: your upper torso, your legs, your abdominals, and your cardiovascular system.

When you're walking, pretend you have a bunch of brightly colored balloons attached to your sternum (the breastbone) and that they are constantly pulling your chest up and out. Hold your head up high, pull your stomach in tight, tighten your buttock muscles, and relax your knees. You will feel light on your feet and have a spring in your step. You will also have perfect posture!

You can carry running shoes in your car and take every available opportunity to go for a brisk walk. Whenever you're in a parking lot, leave your car as far from your destination as possible. If you live in a city and take public transportation, try walking part of the way to work. Inside a building, use the stairs instead of the elevator.

Exercise and Your Daily Life

There are gyms, health clubs, and fitness centers in almost every city where you can use equipment, go to classes, or even get a personal trainer to help you get started on a program that will work best for you.

If you don't like to leave your home to exercise, buy your own treadmill, stationary bicycle, or rowing machine. Or use some of the excellent videocassette programs available for aerobic exercise. There are also some very good books and audiocassette programs available on aerobic exercises that can help you get started on a safe and rewarding program.

Maybe you're fortunate enough to work for one of the hundreds of companies that have started providing their employees with exercise programs. If so, by all means take advantage of it. John Scully, president of the Pepsi-Cola Company, says, "Fitness is the department with the best return on investment."

Question: *It's hard to establish an exercise routine if you travel a lot. Any suggestions?*

Answer: *First, you can pack your running shoes whenever you are going on a trip. Most hotels have jogging maps that give a selection of routes of varying distances. Second, you can book a room in a hotel that is equipped for your needs. More and more hotels worldwide now have swimming pools, workout rooms, and exercise classes available.*

The important thing is to find an exercise program that suits you. As I mentioned, I find it works better for me to go to an early-morning exercise class. Even though I used to teach aerobic dance classes, I don't have the discipline to stay home and work out for an hour by myself. I need the energy of the other people in the class, the structure of a teacher telling me what to do, and the rhythmic music that takes my mind off everything except moving with the beat.

Stocking the Eating Smart Kitchen

Shopping Smart

Shopping smart means making the best food choices when provisioning your kitchen.

The lists at the end of this chapter are very important and can be extremely helpful because they tell you at a glance how to make smart food choices. Throughout the first few chapters I have referred to Preferred and Limited Fuel sources and stressed the importance of choosing foods from the Preferred category whenever possible.

The Preferred Fuels include all of the foods lowest in cholesterol and fat, and highest in fiber.

I have divided the Limited Fuels into two categories: Group A and Group B. Group A Limited Fuels can be used daily, with moderation, to enhance the flavor or texture of the foods on

61

the Preferred list. Group B Limited Fuels are to be used only with great discretion and *only* when they are absolutely necessary for flavor or texture.

I have purposely avoided listing any foods as "forbidden" because I prefer the concept of moderation over martyrdom. Eating Smart is not about deprivation; it is about making better choices.

Since there are about thirty thousand food and nonfood items in most supermarkets, it is easy to become confused when making your selections. To help you in trying to identify preferred commercial brand name items, I recommend *The Living Heart Brand Name Shopper's Guide*, which lists more than five thousand foods low in fat, saturated fat, and dietary cholesterol.

Market Strategy

If you're one of those people who consider going to the market a chore, the grocery industry is doing everything possible to change your mind.

In the nineties the supermarket is rapidly becoming a social gathering place of choice in many suburban areas. People plan to meet at the market for coffee or a glass of wine and do their shopping together. Many stores include delicatessens with attractive dining areas and serve breakfast, lunch, and dinner. Others have coffee gardens in conjunction with bakeries. Some are so glitzy you'd never know you were in a grocery store. The last time I was in a certain supermarket in New Jersey, I thought I'd stepped into a nightclub!

No matter how large or small your own favorite market may be, here are a few of the things that will make shopping trips easier and more fun.

* Schedule your shopping trip just as you would schedule any other important appointment. Allow time for properly storing everything you purchase.

❋ Keep a shopping list on your kitchen wall at all times, and every time you run out of anything, write it on the list. Always include emergency supplies for unexpected occasions, such as dry pasta, rice, canned tuna and clams, and canned tomatoes.

❋ Before going to the market plan your weekly menu and add all the ingredients necessary to your shopping list.

❋ When planning your weekly menu, allow leeway in selection of fresh fruits and vegetables. Wait to choose some of the fresh produce at the market, selecting the best quality available at the time. In-season fruits and vegetables are always the best buy. They look better, have more flavor, and are less expensive.

❋ Never go to the market without a shopping list, and to avoid impulse buying or what's often called "eye-level shopping," stick to your list. This also saves money!

❋ Never shop when you're hungry. If the only time you have available to shop is at the end of the day, have a healthy snack to take the edge off your appetite before marketing. A banana is ideal because it has its own wrapper—just peel and eat! If you're coming right from the office, have a pair of comfortable shoes in your car to change into.

❋ One-stop shopping is not always possible. You may have to go to a health food store for a few of the items you need, such as raw nuts, seeds, and some whole-grain products, or to a fish market for fresh fish and seafood.

Shop the Walls!

Practically all supermarkets are designed the same way. You will find most of the preferred foods on the walls. On one wall are the fresh fruits and vegetables; on another are fresh fish, poultry, and meat; dairy products and basic bread items are also often on the walls.

What does that leave in the middle aisles? The Limited Fuels! There are obvious exceptions to this rule, such as grains, cereals, herbs and spices, some frozen and canned goods, and, of course, cleaning products, paper supplies, pet food, and drug items. The shopping list you take with you to the market should list the items you need in the middle aisles by category so that they are easy to find. Writing your shopping list according to the geographical layout of your market is important for the best use of your time. As soon as you have everything on your list that's in the middle of the market, *run for the walls!*

Read the Labels

Let's start with meat. Be aware of the three main grades: prime, choice, and select or lean. Remember, select contains the least amount of fat and is the least expensive—what a bargain! It is the only thing I know of in today's economy where less money buys you better quality.

Don't allow yourself to be manipulated by clever advertising that tries to turn you into a shopping robot. There are thousands of different food products loaded with fat, sugar, and salt cleverly concealed by misleading labeling. Remember that the word *label* rhymes with *fable*, and you'll find a wealth of storybook nutrition on the labels when you stray from the walls of your supermarket.

For example, the label on a bottle of vegetable oil may list in bold print NO CHOLESTEROL. Of course it has no cholesterol; it never did and it never will. Cholesterol is found only in foods of animal origin. There is no cholesterol in any food or oil of plant origin. The problem is that if Brand A has this label and Brand B doesn't, the average consumer will assume Brand B must have cholesterol. The Food and Drug Administration

(FDA) is working on laws to prevent this from continuing; let's hope they succeed soon.

There are many regulations governing labeling. In fact, they are being revised and updated by the FDA at this very moment. Currently, ingredients must be listed in order of amounts by weight. If you look at a breakfast cereal label and see that the first ingredient listed is sugar, you can be certain the cereal is not a good source of complex carbohydrates. You will find that very few cereals are made of whole grains and very few are made without added sugar. Also, many cereals are very high in sodium.

Other things to watch for on labels are oils and fats. To avoid saturated fat, don't buy any product containing coconut or palm kernel oil. Also avoid buying a product that lists vegetable oil or vegetable shortening as an ingredient since it probably refers to coconut or palm kernel oil. This general terminology allows the manufacturer to use the least expensive oil available without having to change the label.

One of the most misleading areas of labeling is in the fruit juice category. Regulations require that items labeled "fruit juice" be 100 percent real juice; however a "fruit drink" may be primarily sugar with color and flavor added and a small percentage of real juice. Read these labels very carefully.

It is also important to realize that even though salt is not listed as an ingredient, an item may be very high in sodium. The word *sodium* embedded in a larger word (such as mono*sodium* glutamate) should be a tip-off to people on a sodium-restricted diet that the product should be avoided.

Also, try to avoid preservatives. They tend to be the long chemical-sounding words in the ingredients lists. A good rule of thumb is "If the label contains too many words you find difficult to pronounce, don't buy the product."

If you're looking for a bread that is high in fiber, watch out for labeling tricks. Many breads boldly labeled "high in fiber" or "added fiber" are really made with refined flour and just enough bran to use the phrase legally. If the first ingredient listed is anything other than a whole-grain flour, it is not what you are looking for.

Question: *What does "all natural" mean?*

Answer: *Not much. It's a vaguely defined term that suggests a product contains no "artificial" additives and has not been highly processed. It's no guarantee of healthful, nutritious food; a chocolate chip cookie made with white flour, coconut oil, chocolate, and tons of sugar is "all natural."*

Be aware of popular gimmicks in labeling such as "vitamin and mineral fortified" and "all natural." This misleading information can make even junk food appear to be a healthy choice. The sad part is that many of us are actually taken in by these gimmicks and buy the products in good faith. In Jane Brody's *Nutrition Book* she states that "under current law . . . you could fortify cardboard with all the nutrients in wheat cereal and not even have to call it imitation."

Even products labeled "97% fat free" may contain more fat than you want or need. It's the percent of calories from fat that is dangerous. The 3 percent of fat that remains in the "97% fat free" product may constitute nearly 100 percent of the product's calories! Whole milk is only 4 percent butterfat, so you could call it 96 percent fat-free milk!

Another labeling trick to watch for is the small container—

presumably a one-person serving—of a high-fat product with very, very small print that tells you there are "4 servings per container," then gives the nutritional information per serving in large print. Most people assume the calories per serving are for the whole container and not merely one-fourth of its contents.

Restrain yourself while you're shopping. It will make it so much easier for you at home.

All About Storing

Storing everything you purchase as soon as you return home is essential for both the organization of your kitchen and the freshness of your food. It will save you both time and money.

Always keep adequate supplies of material used for proper storage such as plastic bags, wrap, and containers; aluminum foil; and jars with tight-fitting lids. When storing anything in the refrigerator or the freezer, it is important to seal it tightly so that air cannot get to it. This prevents dehydration, which causes loss of taste and texture. Also, unless dairy products are tightly covered in the refrigerator, they will pick up the taste of other foods.

Wash and store all your leafy vegetables and fresh herbs properly, which saves time later. It also saves money because there is less spoilage and it reduces the likelihood of contamination by bugs and bacteria.

All leafy vegetables, such as lettuce, spinach, parsley, basil, and dill, should be torn apart and soaked in cold water until completely free of all dirt and grit. Drain the leaves thoroughly and then roll them up in paper or cotton toweling, or put them in bags before refrigerating them. When you are ready to prepare a salad, your lettuce is clean, crisp, and dry. Dryness is very important because wet lettuce dilutes the salad dressing so that you need more of it.

Question: *Is it true that potatoes will last longer if stored unwashed?*

Answer: *Yes. Root vegetables such as carrots, parsnips, turnips, beets, and potatoes will last longer if stored unwashed in the refrigerator or a cold storage area. Don't peel or scrape them until you're ready to use them.*

People tell me, "Oh, I couldn't possibly take the time when I get home from the market to wash and dry my vegetables before storing them." Do they eat dirty salads? The truth is, you will make healthier choices more frequently when food is already clean and ready to eat than if you have to stop and wash it first.

Before eating fruit, wash it thoroughly to remove any pesticides that may have been sprayed on it. Fruit should not be peeled or cut until you're ready to use it. If the fruit is ripe, put it in the refrigerator to slow down further ripening. If it's not completely ripe, leave it out at room temperature until it is ripe and then refrigerate it. If bananas are getting too ripe, peel and store them in plastic bags in the freezer to use later for milk shakes, cereal toppings, or banana bread.

After opening packages of dried fruits, store them in the refrigerator in covered containers to prevent further dehydration and to keep them fresh and soft longer.

Refrigerate all the natural products your refrigerator will accommodate to ensure their freshness and full flavor for a longer period of time. The oils in many whole grains, nuts, and seeds will quickly turn rancid when not refrigerated.

If you don't use much bread, it is best to keep it in the freezer to be used as needed. Either thaw it at room temperature or put the frozen bread in the toaster to eat immediately.

Canned stock or broth should be kept in the refrigerator so that the fat congeals on the top and can be easily removed after opening.

Tofu (soybean curd) should be refrigerated. After opening the package, place any remaining tofu in fresh water; if you want to add flavor to this nourishing but tasteless food, dice it and store it in fruit juice, stock, or salad dressing.

Arrange your herbs and extracts in a cool place where they are not exposed to sunlight, and alphabetize them for easy access. Alphabetizing may not seem important to you now, but as you acquire more herbs and spices, it will save you time and frustration.

With your groceries organized and properly stored, you are going to find that cooking is a whole lot easier. You'll be amazed at how much less time it takes to assemble the ingredients for a recipe when you know where everything is that you need.

Complex Carbohydrate Foods

Whole-grain products

Breads and rolls
Tortillas (corn or whole wheat)
Grain and cereals (barley, brown rice, buckwheat groats [kasha], cornmeal, popcorn, cracked wheat [bulgur], millet, old-fashioned oatmeal, oat bran, multigrain cereals, and rye)
Cold cereals (shredded wheat, Grape-nuts, and puffed grains such as rice, wheat, corn, and Kashi)

Vegetables

Legumes

(peas and beans, such as lentils, black-eyed peas, chickpeas [garbanzo beans], kidney beans, navy beans, pinto beans, black beans, soybeans, and soybean products such as tofu and tempeh)

Fruits and dried fruits

Animal Protein Foods

Fish

Poultry

skin and all visible fat removed

70

Meat

Buy lean, well-trimmed cuts.

Dairy products

Nonfat milk
Nonfat dry milk powder: available in two forms, instant and noninstant
Evaporated skim milk
Nonfat sour cream
Nonfat yogurt
Nonfat frozen yogurt
Nonfat and low-fat cheese (nonfat or low-fat cottage cheese; nonfat, part-skim, or low-fat ricotta and mozzarella): Use sparingly; high in sodium.
Very low-fat cheese (Romano and Parmesan)
Egg whites: contain no cholesterol or fat
Egg substitute

Frozen Foods

Vegetables

unsalted. Use when fresh vegetables are not available.

Juices and fruits

unsweetened. Use when fresh fruit and fresh fruit juices are not available.

Canned Goods

Vegetables

Use canned when fresh or frozen are not available. Includes tomato products such as tomato sauce, puree, and paste. Also available with no salt added.

Fruits

packed in water or natural juice only, with no sugar added

Fish

tuna and other canned seafood, water-packed. Also available with no salt added.

Stock (chicken or beef)

often called broth: preferable to powder or bouillon cubes. Closer to the flavor of homemade stock and contains less salt. Also available with no salt added. Defat by refrigerating before using and skimming off the fat that rises.

Juices

Fruit: unsweetened only. Use when fresh fruit juices are not available.
Tomato and vegetable: available with no salt added

Seasonings and Condiments

Herbs and spices

both dried and fresh

Extracts

(such as vanilla, coconut, rum, almond, and mint)

Vinegars

all varieties

Tabasco

and other hot sauces

Mustard

(such as Dijon, spicy brown, and horseradish): available in low sodium if necessary

---

Liquid smoke products

Beverages

Water

drinking water, distilled water, sparkling water

Herb tea

caffeine-free (such as orange, mint, cinnamon, and chamomile). A caffeine-free product must be labeled CAFFEINE-FREE.

LIMITED FUELS, GROUP A
(Use Less Frequently)

Carbohydrate Foods

Sugars and syrups

(such as white sugar, brown sugar, fructose, honey, molasses, and maple syrup)

Refined grain products

(such as unbleached flour and white rice)

Animal Protein Foods

Meat

select, not choice or prime grades

Dairy products

Low-fat milk
Buttermilk
Low-fat yogurt
Reduced-fat cheeses (such as cheddar, Monterey Jack, Swiss, and Neufchâtel)
Ice milk
Low-fat frozen yogurt
Low-fat sour cream
Whole eggs (use sparingly)

Plant Protein Foods

Nuts and seeds

Raw nuts (such as almonds, walnuts, and pecans)
Dry roasted unsalted nuts (such as peanuts, cashews, macadamia, and pistachio)
Raw seeds (such as sunflower and sesame)
Unhomogenized (natural, old-fashioned) peanut butter

High-Fat Foods

Margarine

contains no cholesterol but is high in polyunsaturated fat (same calories as butter). Use only pure corn oil, pure canola oil, or pure safflower oil margarines. Read the labels; some less expensive margarines may contain coconut or palm kernel oil, which are saturated fats. Tub margarine is better than stick margarine because it contains less hydrogenated fat.

Oils

Canola
Corn
Cottonseed
Hazelnut
Olive
Peanut
Safflower
Sesame
Soybean
Sunflower
Walnut

High-Fat Foods (continued)

Mayonnaise

> reduced-calorie, no-cholesterol, and no-fat varieties

Condiments

Soy sauce

> reduced-sodium preferred

Worcestershire

> reduced-sodium preferred

Beverages

Coffee

> decaffeinated by water-washed process

Alcohol

> Beer: light varieties preferred
> Liquor: diluted with water or used in cooking
> Wine

LIMITED FUELS, GROUP B
(Use with Great Discretion)

Carbohydrate Foods

Refined grain products

(such as bleached white flour, highly processed and/or sugared cereals, candy, cookies, cakes, and pies)

Animal Protein Foods

Meat

choice and prime grades

High-fat dairy products

Whole milk
Whole yogurt
Half-and-half
Cream
Butter
Sour cream
Ice cream
High-fat cheeses (such as cheddar, Monterey Jack, Swiss, Roquefort, Camembert, Brie, blue, Edam, Liederkranz, Muenster, pimento, and other spreads)
Egg yolks: high in cholesterol and saturated fat. Egg whites are on the Preferred Fuels list because they contain no cholesterol or fat. Whole eggs are on the Group A Limited Fuels list but should be used sparingly.

Plant Protein Foods

Nuts and seeds

> roasted in oil and salted (such as smoked almonds, cocktail peanuts, and sunflower seeds)

Peanut Butter

> homogenized

High-Fat Foods

Oil

> Avoid coconut and palm kernel oils, saturated fats which are also found in many nondairy cream and milk substitutes and some margarines. Also, avoid hydrogenated oils when possible. Read the labels.

Mayonnaise

> regular

Beverages

Coffee

> contains caffeine

Tea

> contains caffeine

Cocoa

contains caffeine, and mixes are high in sugar

Soft drinks

contain sugar and may contain caffeine

Diet sodas

contain artificial sweeteners and may contain caffeine

Miscellaneous

Frozen foods

limit products with added salt, fat, sugar, or preservatives

Canned goods

limit products with added salt, oil, sugar, or preservatives

Catsup

high in sodium and sugar

Olives

high in fat and sodium

Salt

Miscellaneous (continued)

Salt substitutes

>   contain potassium; have a metallic taste when heated

Artificial sweeteners

>   contain chemical additives

Cooking Light, Cooking Right

have always loved to cook. When I first attended cooking
school many years ago, it was so that I could come home and
create elegant and interesting meals for my family and friends.
Initially, that meant lots of butter, aromatic oils, and as much
cream as I needed. Once I became motivated to make everything
I cooked as healthful as it was delicious, cooking became even
more fun—a challenge to achieve the same tastes, textures, and
balance in flavor with as little fat, sugar, and salt as possible.

The successful combination of gastronomy with nutrition is
gratifying because it sets up a win-win situation: You can have
good food that's good for you. In this chapter I'm going to show
you all the tricks and techniques you need to know to create
light, low-fat, and delicious dishes of all types. You will

* use less fat without anyone noticing the difference
* cut down on sugar without giving up sweets
* use less salt without ever missing it

You and your family are also going to discover how much you really like vegetables when they are cooked properly.

The Basics of Low-fat Cooking

When you cook with little or no fat, there is no grease on your stove and no greasy pots and pans to wash. Grease adds work, wastes time, and can clog your arteries and make you fat.

You need to learn a few new techniques or cooking tricks. It may even mean changing some lifelong cooking habits such as frying or sautéing in oil, butter, or margarine. If you follow these five rules, you'll likely enjoy their benefits soon enough to make them your new lifelong habits.

As with calorie and fat counting, the principle here is not deprivation but substitution.

Question: *How much lower in fat is "light" olive oil than regular olive oil?*

Answer: *They are exactly the same. The word "light" in this case refers to flavor, not the amount of fat. "Light" olive oil has practically no taste and can be used in recipes where you don't want the taste of olive oil.*

Question: *Should I use diet margarine?*

Answer: *No. Diet margarine has water blended into it to increase the volume and therefore decrease the calories. If you try to cook with it, you will find it spits water at you. It also tends to make toast soggy.*

WHAT TO WEAR
WHEN COOKING

Always cook in tight-fitting clothes. Tight jeans are ideal. If you wear flowing caftans or big shirts and baggy pants, you'll eventually grow to fit them.

In tight clothes you are much more aware of your body and can more easily avoid the kitchen malady I call "hand-to-mouth disease," which is tasting while you're cooking. A little tasting is necessary, but it's quite common to take in more calories when you're tasting than you would during an average meal.

✳ **Stop frying in fat.** Instead of frying in oil, butter, or margarine, sauté foods in water, stock, juice, or wine. Cook in nonstick cookware or use nonstick spray to prevent sticking and burning.

Among the many tricks that can be used to reduce the amount of fat in cooking, my favorite is to start with onions. They contain so much moisture that when you cook them slowly, the onions "sweat," releasing moisture, so they usually don't need any fat or additional liquid to prevent sticking or burning. You simply chop or slice onions and cook them, covered, over very low heat until the onions are tender. Add a little water or stock only if it becomes necessary to prevent scorching.

After the onions are cooked, add the fish, poultry, meat, other vegetables, or sauce ingredients, and continue cooking just as you would if you had sautéed the onions in oil. When using this method, the onions impart such a wonderful flavor to everything you are cooking with them that no other seasonings are necessary. A good example of a fat-free sauce made by this method of sweating the onions first is Marinara Sauce on page 153.

✳ **Defat stocks and pan drippings.** When using stock, be sure to defat it. If you buy canned stock, store it in the refrigerator and remove the fat before using it. If you make your own stock, be sure to prepare it long enough in advance so that you can refrigerate it until all the fat congeals on the top and can be easily removed. If you're preparing a dish that cooks in liquid, such as pot roast, you can cut down on the fat by refrigerating it overnight, defatting the liquid the next day, and reheating the dish with its fat-free liquid when you're ready to eat it.

This same method for removing fat can be used to obtain fat-free drippings as well. Simply pour the pan drippings into a bowl, place it in the freezer for about twenty minutes, and then scrape off the layer of fat that has accumulated on top. This gives you the basis for fat-free sauces and gravies. The fat-free drippings also add flavor to soups, stews, and casseroles.

* **Thicken with cornstarch, arrowroot, or pureed vegetables.** Classically, most sauces and soups are thickened with a combination of fat and starch, such as butter and flour, which the French call *roux*. It is possible to reduce the calories and fat content of recipes greatly by thickening instead with cornstarch or arrowroot dissolved in water or pureeing vegetables to thicken the rest of the dish. For instance, if you are making a stew, you could thicken it by removing a cup or two of the vegetables, pureeing them in the blender, and returning them to the stew.

* **Substitute low-fat milk for whole milk and cream.** It is possible to make wonderful white or béchamel sauce with nonfat milk. It takes longer to thicken it than when using milk and cream, but the patience pays off in lower-calorie, low-fat sauces.

  Instant nonfat milk powder is a wonderful convenience for busy people. I always tell people it's just like having a cow in your kitchen—you never run out of milk. Mix one-third cup of the dry, nonfat milk with three-fourths cup of water to make one cup of nonfat milk. If you want a creamier consistency for coffee or tea, combine the nonfat dry milk with much less water and still have a nonfat "cream."

* **Cut down on egg yolks.** When you're using eggs, remember the trick is to reduce the amount of egg yolk which has all the fat and cholesterol. Hard-cooked egg whites can be used for garnishing soups, salads, and other dishes. Hard-cooked egg whites can also be stuffed with seasoned, low-fat cheeses or a tofu mixture for delicious, low-cholesterol deviled eggs.

  Beaten raw egg whites substitute surprisingly well for

whole eggs in many recipes. Even scrambled eggs and omelets can be made with only one egg yolk and two or three whites.

Reducing Fat in Fish, Poultry, and Meat

When preparing fish, poultry, or meat, use the following guidelines to reduce the amount of fat in cooking. Before cooking, remove all visible fat from meat and remove the skin of poultry either before cooking or before serving.

Fish

Fish is a good source of animal protein. Many types of fish are lower in fat and, therefore, lower in calories than either poultry or meat.

If you don't think you like fish, chances are that you never had it prepared properly, never had really fresh fish, or both. With modern transportation it's possible to buy fresh fish and shellfish almost everywhere, and they should always be purchased fresh. Fresh fish has clear (not cloudy) eyes and shiny, moist (not dry) scales; and it does not "smell fishy."

Frozen fish can be good if it is thawed properly. The best way to do this is to place the fish in the refrigerator until it's completely thawed. If you want to speed up the process, put the fish in cold water, but never fast-thaw fish by placing it in hot water or by heating it in the oven or microwave. You will totally destroy its texture and wind up with mushy, tasteless fish. Also, never put frozen fish directly on the grill. The fish becomes very dry and tough. This is what sometimes happens in restaurants.

If the fish you order seems dry and has absolutely no taste, you can be sure the fish was frozen and taken out of the freezer and cooked only when you ordered it.

Prepare both fresh and properly thawed fish in exactly the same manner. To avoid the fishy taste that most people find objectionable, first wash the fish in cold water and pat it dry, then place it in a nonaluminum dish and rub a little lemon juice on both sides. If not cooking it immediately, cover and refrigerate.

Fresh, properly prepared fish is delicious without any fatty or creamy sauces. The best way to cook it is to broil, bake, or poach it in stock, water, or wine. Or cook it in onions (see page 84) rather than in oil or butter.

When cooking fish, be very careful not to overcook it. You want the flesh of the fish to go from translucent to opaque but not be dried out and tasteless. Most fish requires only about three minutes of cooking time per side.

Raw fish is also good. Japanese sashimi (sliced raw fish) and sushi (vinegared rice combined with raw fish or seafood) are both popular. Ceviche (the lime-juice-marinated raw-fish Mexican appetizer) is a spicy, tender favorite. Scandinavian gravlax, a cured rather than cooked salmon, is delicious.

Poultry

Poultry is generally a better source of animal protein than meat because its fat can be eliminated by removing the skin and the visible fat.

White meat is lower in fat than dark meat. The white meat of turkey has about as much fat as the white meat of chicken, but the dark meat of turkey is higher in fat than the dark meat of chicken. Domestic duck and goose have 50 percent more fat than chicken. (These comparisons are all based on cooked poultry without skin.) Wild game birds such as pheasant, duck, and quail are also very low in fat but are not readily available to most people.

When cooking poultry on a rack, vertical roaster, or rotisserie where the fat drips away from the meat, it is not necessary to remove the skin until after it is cooked. If you are cooking poultry with other ingredients (such as in a stew or casserole), always remove the skin and visible fat first so that the fat doesn't get mixed into the finished dish; be sure to de-fat prior to eating. The obvious rule here is not to eat the skin or the fat!

Be very careful not overcook poultry, or it will be dry and tough. If you are roasting a chicken for dinner, put it breast side down in a flat roasting pan and bake it at 350°F for about one hour or until the juices run clear when the chicken is pierced with a knife.

If you are planning to chop up the chicken later to use in another dish such as chicken salad, remove it from the oven while the juices are still running a little pink. The chicken will continue to cook as it cools and will be more moist and have more flavor.

When sautéing chicken breasts, cook them only until they turn from translucent to opaque. When they spring back to the touch, they are done, moist and tender. This takes only a few minutes per side.

Don't allow poultry to sit at room temperature for too long. All types of poultry, as well as eggs, quickly build up harmful bacteria when not refrigerated. This is also true of foods containing poultry or eggs such as mayonnaise and hollandaise sauce.

When freezing chicken or other poultry, I prefer to leave the skin on. Freezing tends to dehydrate everything, so leaving the skin on poultry helps to protect it against dryness.

Red Meat

The leanest (least fat-marbled) cuts of meat include flank and round steak, lean lamb or pork loin, and veal. Interestingly enough, while veal is lower than beef in fat content, it is higher in cholesterol. Organ meats such as liver are also low in fat but extremely high in cholesterol. All organ meats are high in vitamins and minerals but should be limited in your diet because of their high cholesterol content. Wild game such as venison and elk are also sources of lean meat because they have not been confined in small spaces to prevent them from losing weight.

Always buy the leanest cuts of meat you can find, and if possible, grind your own meat for hamburgers and meatloaf; that way you can better control the fat content.

Carefully remove all visible fat when preparing meat. Use cooking methods, such as baking and broiling on a rack, that allow the fat to drain away from the meat. Marinating tougher cuts of meat, such as flank steak, will make them more tender. Try my Marinade recipe on page 150.

Try to make stews and soups the day before you plan to serve them so that you have time to refrigerate them overnight and remove any congealed fat. An added bonus is the superior flavor of reheated soups and stews.

Cooking time is not as crucial with meat as it is with poultry and fish. Although many cuts of meat improve in taste and texture when served rare, there are many other cuts, such as rump roast and stew meat, that improve in taste and texture when cooked for long periods of time.

Treat all meat as a side dish or even a condiment rather than the main course. You might think of it as a supporting actor rather than the star of the show. Serve small portions: Animal protein should never be more than one-fifth the volume of your meal.

Reducing Sugar

It is possible to reduce the amount of sugar you use in cooking without giving up sweetness. You can raise the level of perceived sweetness in many foods without adding any sweetener by using vanilla extract, cinnamon, or both. Try this experiment: Put one teaspoon of vanilla extract and a sprinkle of cinnamon in a glass of milk and ask someone to tell you if it has sugar in it. The person will almost always say yes because the milk tastes so much sweeter.

The level of sweetness in many fruits can be increased by cooking them, which concentrates the carbohydrates. Broiling a sliced or lengthwise-halved banana until it's bubbling and starting to brown makes it so sweet you can use it for jam. It's also fabulous on cooked cereal in place of sugar. Or try broiling a halved grapefruit. It will become much sweeter and is a delightful variation for both breakfast and dessert.

Question: *Can I substitute frozen concentrated fruit juice for the sugar called for in recipes?*

Answer: *You can substitute it only for another liquid in the recipe. For example, no liquid is usually called for in cookie recipes; therefore, you would ruin the texture of the cookie by adding fruit juice.*

You can usually reduce the amount of sugar called for in any recipe by at least one-third and often as much as one-half. You can always reduce the measurement called for by at least one-third if you substitute pure crystalline fructose for ordinary table sugar. Fructose, which is one and one-half times sweeter, is available in most supermarkets and in all health food stores. It can be used instead of sugar in all recipes except those for candy (fructose doesn't make candy harden properly). This one drawback should be of little consequence to you since you aren't likely to be making candy very often if you're Eating Smart!

For everyday desserts, fresh fruit, served either raw or cooked, is the best choice. When you want to prepare a special-occasion treat, there are many wonderful low-calorie, low-fat, sugar-free dessert books you can use. Read some of them for ideas and then start creating your own desserts. Moreover, new "light" baked goods appear in our markets almost daily.

Pureed fresh fruits make wonderful sauces and dressings for other fruits, angel food cake, or a "light" pound cake. Or make your own fresh fruit yogurt dessert: Buy plain nonfat yogurt without sugar or honey, then add a little vanilla extract, a dash of cinnamon, and the fresh fruit of your choice.

Remember, when you revise a high-fat, high-calorie recipe to make it lower in fat and calories, it does not become calorie-free. A guest at the Canyon Ranch told me she loved my "light" cheesecake recipe so much that every time she made it, she ate the whole thing.

Reducing Salt

I call salt the great dietary whitewash. If something doesn't taste quite right, people add salt! Actually, if your food is seasoned just right, you don't need the salt. Most Americans use five times more salt than is recommended by the American Heart Association.

Our taste buds pick up only four basic tastes: sweet, salt, sour, and bitter. Each of these tastes is sensed by a band of taste buds on a specific area of the tongue. The first band of taste buds, on the tip of the tongue, is for sweet; the second for salt; the third for sour; and the fourth, at the back of the tongue, is for bitter.

If I blindfolded you, handed you an ice cream cone, and asked you to lick it with the tip of your tongue and then tell me if it was sweet, you would say yes. If I handed you a dill pickle and asked you to lick it with the tip of your tongue and then tell me if it was sour, you would say no because the sour taste buds are much farther back on your tongue.

Have you ever noticed that when a person tastes something really bitter, he'll grimace as if he's gagging? This is because the bitter taste buds are the farthest back on the tongue.

If our tongues can taste only sweet, salt, sour, and bitter, then how do we savor all the great food tastes we love? We smell them. Because we taste and smell at the same time, we're able to enjoy so many different flavors in our food. You have proved this to yourself whenever you've had a bad cold. You probably told people you could not taste. More accurately, you couldn't *smell* because your nose was stopped up. Therefore, nothing tasted as you expected it to taste. In fact, food probably didn't have much flavor at all.

What does all this prove? You can reduce salt in your cooking and heighten flavor by making your food smell better. Herbs and spices do the job beautifully. Also, stock, juices, or wine can replace water for added flavor or smell in cooking.

Deliberately stimulating the other taste buds will keep you from missing salt, too. For instance, you can add something sweet (such as fructose or concentrated fruit juice) or something sour (such as fresh lemon juice or vinegar). For the few things you feel you cannot eat without salt, try adding just a pinch—literally a few grains—of fructose and a very few drops of fresh lemon juice. You'll find that not only do you not miss the salt, but food such as celery sticks and eggs will taste fresher, more interesting, and more flavorful.

After you have started consciously reducing the amount of added salt in your food, you actually lose your taste for it. Canned soups and soups served in most restaurants will taste as if they've been made with salt water.

There's another wonderful benefit to salt-free cooking. It's the salt in the dressing, not the other ingredients, that wilts the greens. Did you know that you can toss a salad with a salt-free dressing several hours before serving without the greens wilting at all?

Herbs and Spices

Herbs and spices are extremely important in the Eating Smart approach to cooking. They contain practically no calories and greatly enhance the flavor of food. Used liberally, they compensate for salt.

When using dried herbs and spices that are not powdered, it is essential to crush them using a mortar and pestle to release their full aroma.

When you begin using more herbs and spices in your cooking, you will be amazed at how much better everything tastes. Salad dressings, sauces, and casseroles will have a fuller, more satisfying flavor with appreciably less or no salt added. Everyone will ask you where you have been taking cooking classes!

A number of good herb mixtures now on the market are completely free of salt and provide interesting flavors for all types of dishes. Look for them in your grocery store.

Remember — smell equals flavor!

It's also fun to grow your own fresh herbs. Most nurseries carry small plants, or you can even buy seeds and start from scratch. Fresh herbs not only enhance the flavor of many foods, they also make unusual and attractive garnishes for plates.

You can change the whole character of a recipe by using different herbs and spices. For example, you can take a basic chicken recipe and change the flavor to Italian by adding oregano, to Oriental by adding a little curry powder and ginger, or to southwestern by adding ground cumin and chili powder. You are limited only by your imagination when it comes to recipe development and menu planning, so start experimenting and have fun.

New Ways with Vegetables

Vegetables are truly God's gift of health to all, and they are essential to the Eating Smart approach to cooking. Vegetables are beautiful, delicious, high in vitamins and minerals, and low in calories. They are also high in fiber and contain some protein. Most people who think they don't like vegetables have probably never really had fresh vegetables or properly cooked vegetables.

Raw vegetables, such as carrots, celery, radishes, tomatoes, lettuces, cabbage, and sprouts of all types, make wonderful hors d'oeuvres, snacks, and salads, and many vegetables not normally served raw, such as broccoli, cauliflower, turnips, parsnips, and asparagus, are also delicious that way.

Steaming is the best method for cooking vegetables because

when they are cooked above the water level, none of their nutrients are discarded in the cooking liquid. By following the recommended cooking times on the steaming chart (pages 96–97), you will preserve the maximum amount of nutrients available. Prolonged cooking tends to destroy water-soluble vitamins.

There are many types of steamers available, but all you need is a collapsible steamer basket and a pot with a lid. Place enough water in the pot to bring the level to just below the steamer basket, bring the water to a rapid boil, and put the vegetable in the basket. Cover the pot and set your timer, using the steaming chart as a guide.

As soon as the vegetable has cooked, remove the steamer from the pot and place it under cold running water. This stops the cooking process and preserves both the color and the texture of the vegetable. At this point you may wish to refrigerate the vegetable to serve cold or to reheat later.

Q
&
A

Question: *Can canned tomatoes be used as a substitute for ripe tomatoes?*

Answer: *Yes. As a matter of fact, when really tasty ripe tomatoes are not in season, canned tomatoes often offer more flavor. Also, a little tomato paste can be added to fresh tomatoes for more flavor.*

When reheating vegetables, be careful not to overcook them. I like to reheat vegetables in a little stock mixed with crushed

STEAMING TIMES
FOR
FRESH VEGETABLES

The time given for steaming each vegetable produces a crisp-tender result. Mushy, colorless vegetables not only are tasteless but have been robbed of much of their nutritional value by overcooking.

Vegetable	Minutes		
Artichokes	30	Celery stalks	10
Asparagus	5	Chard	1 to 2
Beans		Chayote	3
Green	5	Chicory	1 to 2
Lima	5	Chives	2 to 3
String or snap	5	Collards (stems removed)	1 to 2
Bean sprouts	1 to 2	Corn	
Beet greens	3 to 5	Kernels	3
Beets, quartered	15	On the cob	3
Breadfruit	10	Cucumber	2 to 3
Broccoli	5	Dandelion greens	1 to 2
Brussels sprouts	5	Eggplant, cut up	5
Cabbage, quartered	5	Garlic	5
Carrots, ½-inch slices	5	Jerusalem artichokes	8
Cauliflower		Jicama	10
Florets	3	Kale	1 to 2
Whole	5	Kohlrabi, quartered	8 to 10
Celery root	3 to 4	Leeks	5

Vegetable		Minutes
Lettuce	1 to 2	
Lotus root, ¼-inch slices	25	
Mushrooms	2	
Mustard, fresh	1 to 2	
Okra	5	
Onions		
Green tops	3	
Whole	5	
Palm hearts	5	
Pea pods	3	
Peas	3 to 5	
Peppers		
Chiles	2 to 3	
Green and red bell	2	
Pimientos	2	
Potatoes		
Sweet, ½-inch slices	15	
White, ½-inch slices	10	
Pumpkin, cut up		5
Radishes, black, ½-inch slices		5
Radishes, red		5
Rhubarb		5
Rutabagas		8
Shallots		2
Spinach		1 to 2
Squash		
Acorn, cut up		5
Hubbard, cut up		5
Summer		3
Zucchini		3
Tomatoes		3
Turnips, quartered		8
Water chestnuts		8
Watercress		1 to 2

herbs. Just put the stock and herbs in a saucepan, bring to a boil, add the vegetables, and heat to desired temperature.

People have told me that they do not like cooking cabbage, cauliflower, and broccoli because these vegetables emit an odor that permeates the house. The fact is, if you can smell them cooking, they are already overcooked. Use the steaming chart that follows, and you'll never have to worry about the smell of cabbage in your kitchen again!

I routinely steam most vegetables for one to two minutes, or blanch them in boiling water, even if I am serving them "raw." The color is more intense and the texture is better for dipping.

Cooked vegetables can be the basis for fast, delicious meals such as vegetables au gratin. Put them in a baking dish, sprinkle a bit of grated low-fat cheese over the top, and heat them until the vegetables are hot and the cheese is melted.

You can also stir-fry vegetables in a wok or large skillet. Instead of oil, use water, de-fatted stock, juice, or wine. When stir-frying, it is important to cut the vegetables in approximately the same size pieces for even cooking. Those that take the longest to cook should be placed in the wok or skillet first. Cutting the vegetables diagonally improves the appearance of the finished dish.

Microwave ovens are also wonderful for cooking vegetables. Just cover the vegetables to be cooked and follow the timing directions for your oven.

The vegetables we usually think of baking are potatoes, sweet potatoes, yams, squash, and onions. It is possible, however, to bake any kind of vegetable and give it a character totally different from what it would have if cooked another way. You can add greatly to the flavor of a vegetable by baking it in a little de-fatted stock, juice, or wine. Try adding your favorite herbs and spices, too. Baked vegetables are also good cold in salads or served as side dishes.

Broiling or grilling vegetables is another excellent method for cooking them with very little added fat. I like them best brushed lightly with a very good extra-virgin olive oil while they're cooking. Sliced peppers, eggplant, squash, and all root vegetables are good grilled.

The All-Purpose Potato

Potatoes are particularly versatile vegetables. Baked potatoes seasoned with herbs and spices are good side dishes and also make wonderful entrees when stuffed with other ingredients. They are also delicious served with fat-free gravy, which adds almost no calories or fat to the potato. The recipe for Fat-Free Gravy is on page 149.

Stuffed baked potatoes make fast, nutritious meals and are a wonderful way to use leftovers. I consider myself somewhat of an expert in the potato-stuffing field because I wrote a book titled *Stuffed Spuds, 100 Meals in a Potato*. Believe me, I could practically scoop them out and stuff them in my sleep when I finished that book!

My favorite stuffed spud is one I named the Runner's Spud. Potato pulp is mixed with low-fat cottage cheese, chopped apples, raisins, and toasted sunflower seeds, and is served cold. It's a great snack or a wonderful brown-bag lunch.

Russets are the best potatoes for stuffing because they have a fairly thick skin. You bake them in a 400°F oven for an hour or so, and when they're cool enough to handle, cut a slice off the top and carefully remove the pulp and mash it. Then mix it with whatever you have and stuff it back into the potato shell. Either reheat it, serve it at room temperature, or refrigerate and serve it cold.

You can make fat-free French "fries" by a method I call oven-frying. Cut the potatoes in strips, spray them with nonstick spray, and bake them in a 375°F oven for an hour, turning them occasionally so they'll brown evenly.

Baked yams and sweet potatoes are also handy for snacks as

JAMES BEARD'S OVERBAKED POTATO

I still remember my amazement years ago when James Beard told me about his "overbaked potato." He claimed he baked a potato for two hours at 450°F. I thought I had misunderstood him, but he assured me the potato was sensational this way—like a puff pastry shell on the outside, creamy in the middle, and best seasoned only with freshly ground black pepper. I tried it immediately and agreed. It is delicious! However, I like it served with not only freshly ground black pepper but also a dash of freshly grated Parmesan or Romano cheese.

well as meals. They are so sweet and satisfying, they don't need anything on them; it's not possible to improve their wonderful natural taste.

But go easy on the quantity. When I was developing recipes and designing menus at the Pritikin Longevity Center in Santa Monica, we served baked yams, cut in half, as afternoon snacks. One guest who was trying to lose weight told me she had *gained* two pounds during the first week. When I started talking to her about what she was eating, I found out that she was routinely eating the equivalent of three or four baked yams every afternoon and sometimes taking a few more back to her room as a bedtime "snack." She had missed the point. The idea was to teach the participants that you could substitute a really healthy, sweet, and satisfying food like a yam for a sweet roll or a cookie, not that baked yams were a "free" food!

Baked yams are so sweet that they make wonderful desserts simply pureed and scooped into sherbet glasses like pudding. If you have children, keep a baked yam or two in the refrigerator for after-school snacks. Kids love them!

Salad Savvy

A salad does not have to be a boring combination of lettuce and tomatoes tossed with dressing and served on chilled plates. Warm or hot-and-cold salads are exciting. Combining different textures by adding croutons, nuts, and seeds to your salads also adds interest. A salad can be small, practically calorie-free, and served as a first course or as a side dish. It can also be made larger and contain a variety of ingredients suitable for an entree or main course.

My favorite hot-and-cold salad is made by cooking sliced fresh mushrooms in Fat-Free Dressing until they are tender, and then spooning the hot mushroom dressing mixture over a combination of greens such as spinach, romaine, arugula, endive, or escarole. Watch the faces of your guests when they take the first bite—they will be delightfully surprised! See Hot Mushroom Fat-Free Dressing (page 145).

An even more elaborate version of this salad can be made by sprinkling a little low-fat cheese on the greens before spooning over the hot dressing. Then top the salad with some chopped, toasted nuts.

Other vegetables can also be cooked in Fat-Free Dressing (page 144) and spooned over a salad. This is not only delicious but sometimes it's also practical. Let's say you were planning to use sliced carrots in a salad but found they were limp and tired-looking. Just peel them, slice them thinly, cook them in the dressing until fork-tender, and spoon them over the salad. You will appear to be a culinary genius rather than someone caught at the last minute with wilted vegetables.

Salads can also be made with fruits, fish, poultry, meat, pastas of all kinds, rice, bulgur, or any other grain.

Sprouts of all kinds are good in salads and make beautiful plate garnishes. Growing your own sprouts is fun, easy, and economical. Seeds vary greatly in their sprouting times and yields. Alfalfa is by far the fastest-growing, but there are many others, and any health food store should be able to give you information if you're interested.

When it comes to salad dressing, it is always better to make your own. It will have a better flavor, contain no preservatives, and be much less expensive than bottled dressings. Classic salad dressing has a ratio of three parts oil to one part vinegar. Only a fraction of this amount of oil is necessary to make the dressing cling to the greens. Prepare your own favorite dressing recipe, using only a few tablespoons of oil instead of a cup or two and substituting water for the difference in volume. It's fun to experiment with different vinegars and oils; try combinations such as rice vinegar and sesame oil, raspberry vinegar and walnut oil, or balsamic vinegar and extra-virgin olive oil. Or completely

STUFFED
POTATOES

You can stuff potatoes with almost anything.
Some possibilities:

Chili and fat-reduced cheddar cheese

Sauerkraut and fat-reduced Swiss
cheese (a Reuben potato)

Banana and unhomogenized peanut
butter (weird but fantastic)

Lean Ground beef, taco sauce, lettuce,
tomato, and cilantro

Sautéed onion, cooked skinless
chicken breast, potato pulp, and a
sprinkling of Parmesan cheese

Borscht or vichyssoise

Potato pulp combined with hoop
cheese and buttermilk, seasoned
with parsley, dill, and Dijon mustard (very low-fat)

eliminate the oil by making the simple, tasty Fat-Free Dressing on page 144.

Legumes of All Types

Legumes, which include all dried beans and peas, are inexpensive and high in vitamins, minerals, and fiber. They are an excellent source of plant protein when served with a grain, such as beans with corn or whole wheat flour tortillas, or black-eyed peas with rice.

I call tofu, or soybean curd, the recipe chameleon. It basically has no flavor. You can marinate it in salad dressing, stock, or fruit juice, and it will take on any flavor you desire. It is also perfect for adding body to sauces and dressings of all types. Other soybean products include textured vegetable protein (such as tempeh, bacon and sausage substitutes, and soy "burgers"). These soybean products are free of cholesterol and very low in saturated fats, of course, but many of them are very high in sodium, so check the labels before buying them.

Pasta — Hot or Cold

Pasta is versatile, easy to prepare, and inexpensive. Prehistoric humans discovered that grains had to be cooked in order to make them into a paste, which then became one of their main food sources. Later on, after someone discovered how to make dumplings by cooking this paste in boiling water, it was natural to hit upon the idea of flattening out the dumplings and forming them into different shapes: pasta!

The Chinese are credited with the first noodles, but Italy has more kinds of pasta than any other country—spaghetti, linguine, fettuccine, lasagna, rotelli, rotini, tortellini, macaroni, ravioli, vermicelli, and on and on. More and more pastas are becoming staples on our menus.

When cooking pasta, remember the Italian guideline, *al dente*, which literally means "to the tooth," slightly resistant to the bite. Overcooking pasta until it is soft and soggy will ruin an otherwise wonderful pasta dish, so make sure to follow package directions and test frequently. Whole wheat pasta has to be served at once because it gets gummy when it stands for any length of time.

You can buy whole wheat pasta and vegetable pastas in gourmet markets and specialty health food stores. The vegetable pastas are regular pasta with enough of the vegetable added for color and a bit of flavor. In pasta shops which are springing up all over the country you can buy fresh pastas of all types. You might even enjoy making your own. It's relatively easy and lots of fun. You can make it with or without a pasta machine.

Because pasta is so versatile, you can let your imagination run wild, and because it's inexpensive, you can enjoy it often. Pastas combine well with leftovers or all types, and most dishes are good hot or cold. There are lots of new pasta cookbooks. It's easy to modify the recipes in them or to modify your own favorites just by omitting or reducing the amount of oil and salt called for and replacing the high-fat ingredients with low-fat ones.

Keep pasta on hand for emergency meals. You can feed lots of people on the spur of the moment with a made-in-minutes pasta meal and look like a super chef.

Fat-Free Beverages

Fat-free beverages can taste sensational. Shakes made with ⅔ cup of nonfat milk and fruit are delicious, creamy, and naturally refreshing. Just freeze the fruit you plan to use and then combine it with an equal amount of nonfat milk in a blender. In fact, a tasty cereal topping is actually a banana shake: nonfat milk blended with half a frozen banana. I like it better than bananas sliced over the top of the cereal because the fruit flavor permeates the whole bowl.

Cold melon can be pureed until it's liquid and then served in chilled glasses garnished with a sprig of mint. Add a little soda water for a sparkling melon cooler.

For the holidays, surprise your friends with a fat-free Sugar-Free White Eggnog (page 166). It is white because you omit the egg yolk for a lower-cholesterol beverage. For nonalcoholic eggnog use rum or brandy extracts.

Low-Fat Snacks

Low-fat snacks are fine alternatives to what a friend of mine refers to as "salted fat": potato chips, corn chips, commercial popcorn, and all the rest of the packaged, inferior fuel Americans love to nibble.

Popcorn is a superb snack when prepared without oil and served with little or no salt. You can pop your own popcorn without oil either in a hot air popper or in a heavy iron skillet with a lid. A large, heavy saucepan will also serve the purpose;

just shake it continuously while the corn is popping. My own favorite way to serve popcorn is with a hint of curry powder. Before you decide I'm crazy, try it. Remember, just a little! Curry powder goes a long way, and your guests should not even be able to guess what it is. If you want to add a little oil, try olive oil—it's delicious on popcorn.

To make your own tasty tortilla chips, just cut whole corn tortillas into snack-size pieces and bake them in a 350°F oven for about fifteen minutes, until crisp, turning them over so both sides will brown. Sprinkle with a tiny bit of salt (or none at all) and lime juice.

You can turn garbanzo beans into low-fat garbanzo nuts by cooking them until they are tender, then baking them until they are crunchy. The recipe is on page 163.

To enhance the flavor of raw nuts and seeds so that smaller amounts are adequate, toast them just before using them. Toasted nuts and seeds are good in salads and on top of some entrees for both flavor and texture, but their use should be limited because they are high in fat. Toast them in a 350°F oven for about eight minutes. Watch them carefully because they burn easily.

Do It Yourself

I could go on and on with additional tips and techniques, but you get the idea. My purpose is to impart the basics so that you can apply them to your own life as you see fit. If you follow the principles and techniques of Eating Smart, no cookbook or recipe will be off-limits. You can revise other people's recipes to make them healthful; you can enjoy any of the thousands of wonderful cookbooks published each year; you can forever create food that's good and good for you.

Five-to-One Formula Menus

8

You don't need to compute calories or find fat grams when you're using the Five-to-One Formula for your menu planning. You don't need to follow set menus ever again. Just plan your meals around the things you like best, adapt them to comprise at least five times as much in volume of carbohydrate foods as animal protein foods, and keep high-fat foods to a minimum.

If you want to splurge with your favorite sauce at dinner, you can. Just be careful about how much high-fat dressing you use on the salad. Remember, your goal is to keep your fat calories around 20 percent of the total calories each day—not to achieve a fat-free diet.

Likewise, you're not planning hospital menus. You are planning healthful Five-to-One Formula menus that allow you to enjoy food as *food* even as you eat it as fuel. The objective in Eating Smart is not deprivation but learning how to fuel the

> *Five-to-One Formula menu planning is just the reverse of traditional menu planning: You don't plan a chicken dinner, you plan to have some chicken with your dinner.*

mind and body for maximum performance and at the same time enjoy sumptuous, delicious meals that truly satisfy the soul.

When you're planning weekly menus, strive for variety in taste and types of food as well as good nutritional balance. It's fun to experiment with recipes of ethnic and regional origins. For example, you could have a Mexican dinner one night with burritos or fajitas, an Oriental dinner with teriyaki tuna or a vegetable entree stir-fried in a wok another night, and then an Italian dinner of linguine with clam sauce or any other pasta with vegetables later on in the week.

Plate Appeal

When planning meals, visualize how the food is going to look on the plates. You want a colorful combination of foods that is eye-catching and inviting. For example, you might like chicken, cauliflower, and mashed potatoes, but if you put all three on the same dinner plate, it is certainly not going to look very appealing. However, if you serve carrots, asparagus, or broccoli instead of the cauliflower, and sprinkle a little paprika and chopped parsley on the potato, the plate will be colorful and much more exciting.

You can also add more interest to a meal when your foods

have a variety of textures. You wouldn't want to serve creamed tuna with a pureed vegetable and mashed potatoes. If you're going to serve the creamed tuna, serve it with chopped vegetables cooked crisp-tender and maybe a baked potato or oven "fries."

Planning Ahead

When planning your weekly menus, consider your time. Prepare as many dishes as possible in advance and always build in a couple of "catch-up" meals. That's when you use up everything you have left over from the two or three previous days. The French turn leftovers, mixed with cooked white beans, into a kind of casserole called a cassoulet. You can do the same thing with your leftovers, using the same white beans the French use or other kinds of legumes, pasta, or rice.

Starting Your Day

A friend of mine, a writer, was getting ready to go on a big book tour. He was desperately trying to lose weight before his appearance on the "Today Show" and asked me if I would have breakfast with him to give him some pointers.

He ordered a croissant. I asked, "Why eat a croissant?" He told me it was because he didn't miss butter on croissants. I should hope not! A croissant is 50 percent butter by weight.

When it comes time for breakfast, dare to be different. The classic American breakfast of bacon and eggs should be history. Unfortunately, it is still the daily fare for millions of people who run on Limited Fuel. For millions more, each day begins with a sweet roll or a couple of doughnuts and a cup of coffee—more Limited Fuel.

And there are those who try to start the day without any fuel intake at all. This latter group always reminds me of my favorite cartoon that shows a grossly overweight, miserable-looking man, framed by the caption, "People who try to lose weight by skipping breakfast end up fat and mean!"

Most diet book menu plans give you one breakfast for an entire week and then just say "Repeat." I get bored with the same thing every morning, and I'll bet you do, too. So use your imagination and experiment with some breakfast ideas of your own.

For example, try putting your favorite low-fat cheese such as ricotta, mozzarella, or cottage cheese on a toasted whole wheat bagel or English muffin, then top it with Apple Butter (page 152) or thinly sliced fresh fruit. It's delicious!

You can make wonderful omelets using only one egg yolk and two or three egg whites. My favorite is the southwestern

Question: *Is it true that eating grapefruit burns up cholesterol?*

Answer: *No. Some smart grapefruit grower probably started this rumor as a marketing gimmick.*

omelet with tomatoes, onions, and green chiles, which I serve
with hot tortillas.

To help you get started, here is a week's worth of possible
breakfasts (recipes begin on page 141):

1. ■ Shredded wheat; fresh or fresh frozen strawberries;
   non-fat milk
2. ■ Breakfast sandwich made with whole wheat toast or
   bagel; Breakfast Cheese (recipe); Apple Butter (recipe)
3. ■ Melon or papaya omelet made with 1 egg whole and 2
   egg whites; salsa; corn tortillas
4. ■ Whole wheat pancakes or waffle; broiled banana;
   Breakfast Cheese (recipe)
5. ■ Broiled grapefruit; whole wheat English muffin with
   melted fat-reduced cheese such as 20 percent fat-
   reduced Swiss or cheddar
6. ■ Oatmeal or grits with raisins or dried prunes; Yogurt
   Sauce (recipe)
7. ■ Banana-Bran Shake (recipe) for when you're really in a
   hurry!

When you're not at home and in control of what you eat, all
is not lost. You can pick and choose from the food available to
have a tasty and nutritious breakfast. One morning, for instance,
I had breakfast in a coffee shop where absolutely nothing on
the menu reflected a "healthy start." Even the dry cereals were
all sugar-frosted! After reading the menu through twice, I ordered pancakes with grilled bananas and cottage cheese. The
waitress told me they didn't have grilled bananas. I suggested
that the cook spoon the sliced bananas on top of the pancake
batter after he poured the pancakes on the grill; that way the
bananas would cook right along with the pancakes.

As soon as my "banana pancakes" arrived, I put the cottage
cheese between the hot pancakes so it would melt into them.

The bananas made them so sweet, I didn't need syrup, and the cottage cheese replaced the butter. Even the waitress told me how good my breakfast looked!

My point is that with a little imagination and armed with the knowledge of what you want, you can usually come up with something that is easy for the cook and much better for you than any menu item.

The Middle of the Day

Eating Smart on the Job

Five-to-One Formula lunches can be made easily portable and taken with you to work. In fact, I have found that high-quality fuel is actually more practical for brown bagging. Whole-grain breads have a firmer, more interesting texture than refined white bread, so sandwiches stay fresher and taste good for a longer period of time. Less butter, margarine, or mayonnaise on sandwiches keeps them from getting soggy. Raw vegetables and fresh whole fruits are easily packed to go, and so are small cartons of nonfat or low-fat cottage cheese and yogurt.

Dried fruits make marvelous snacks to carry with you in a handbag or briefcase, or to keep in your desk or car. Throw in a bottle of sparkling water, a small bottle of angostura bitters, and a wedge of lemon or lime, and you can even enjoy a Pilot's Cocktail (page 33) with your lunch!

Brown-bag lunches are becoming more and more popular with both office workers and people who must spend a lot of time driving because of their job requirements. It is estimated that over forty million workers in the United States carry lunch to work each day. And even though brown bagging has obvious money-saving advantages, recent research shows that families who brown-bag it tend to have more money (and be better educated) than those who don't.

Packing your lunch not only saves you money but gives you extra time for other activities on your lunch break, such as exercise, shopping, letter-writing, or getting to your next destination in your car. It also allows you to directly control the quality and quantity of your meal.

Last year over $46 billion was spent in food stores on brown-bag lunch ingredients. With this rising popularity of the portable meal, manufacturers are coming out with many new convenience products. A good example is the cold box: a plastic container with a lid you freeze. It will keep food cold for up to five hours. They come in all sizes, from small containers for individual portions to ones that will hold several sandwiches or a complete meal. There are also compartmentalized lunch boxes available with several plastic containers for different types of foods and beverages.

Question: *What can I use to replace mayonnaise in potato and tuna salads?*

Answer: *Use either nonfat mayonnaise or nonfat yogurt, or make your own mayonnaise substitute following the recipe on page 148.*

Here are seven sample lunches you can make yourself or order from a menu in a restaurant (recipes begin on page 141):

1. ■ Turkey salad, Fat-Free Dressing (recipe), whole wheat roll or toast, and sliced orange. (If ordering in a restaurant and they don't have turkey salad on the menu, order a chef's salad and tell them to hold the ham and cheese—you want only the turkey! Ask for the dressing on the side and use only a little bit of it.)
2. ■ Fruit and cottage cheese salad; toasted bagel
3. ■ Pasta with fresh vegetables; melon
4. ■ Carrot salad; Canyon Ranch Stuffed Spud (recipe); fresh fruit
5. ■ Bean Burritos (recipe); salsa; pineapple, fresh or canned in unsweetened juice
6. ■ Vegetable pizza; fresh fruit
7. ■ Lean hamburger on whole wheat bun; tomato; sliced onion; Thousand Island Dressing (recipe); fresh fruit

The Evening Meal

At the end of the day most people want to relax and enjoy a leisurely meal. It is often the only time of the day when the entire family can eat together. Dinner is also the most popular time for entertaining. Whether you are planning dinner for your family and friends or just cooking for yourself, preparation time may be a big factor.

The following dinner menu suggestions can be used as guidelines for your own meal planning. Variations on any theme are endless. Just use these as a starting point (recipes begin on page 141):

1. ■ Lettuce and tomato salad; Fat-Free Dressing (recipe); lean broiled steak; baked potato with fat-free sour cream and chives; Cherry Trifle (recipe)
2. ■ Orange (or fresh fruit) and onion salad; fresh fish (broiled, baked, or poached); steamed broccoli; rice pudding or fresh fruit
3. ■ Coleslaw; barbecued chicken; corn on the cob; Pumpkin Mousse (recipe) or fresh fruit
4. ■ Spinach salad; Hot Mushroom Fat-Free Dressing (recipe); broiled lamb chops; rice pilaf with vegetables; berries with Yogurt Sauce (recipe)
5. ■ Grilled vegetables; Linguine with Clam Sauce (recipe); fresh fruit sorbet
6. ■ Egg drop soup; vegetable stir-fry; brown rice; pineapple (fresh or packed in juice)
7. ■ Salad of young greens; Raspberry Walnut Vinaigrette Dressing (recipe); fish and vegetable kabobs; barley pilaf; baked apple

Coping with
Challenges

ost restaurants serve portions designed for men well over six feet tall and weighing over two hundred pounds. Most airlines serve high-fat meals, cocktails, coffee, and very little water. When you're someone else's guest, you feel guilty if you don't eat the high-fat fare being offered. When you're the host or hostess, you are afraid your guests will think you are cheap or strange if you don't serve large portions of fish, poultry, or meat.

This chapter is intended to help you cope with the challenges modern life throws in the way of those devoted to Eating Smart—challenges such as dining in restaurants; traveling as a necessary part of life; being entertained by personal friends, family, and business associates; and entertaining all of these groups yourself. I hope that these suggestions will make dining out a pleasant experience and jet lag a thing of the past; that you will no longer feel guilty telling either your boss or Aunt Tilda that you simply couldn't finish the apple pie because you had already eaten too much of the delicious meal; and that the most sought-after invitations in town will be to your parties.

Eating Smart in Restaurants

Eating in a restaurant is not only an enjoyable event but a way of life for many people. You won't feel as if you need to deny yourself anything when dining out if you follow a few simple guidelines.

* **Order all of your sauces and salad dressings served on the side.** By doing this you don't miss the opportunity of tasting a particularly delicious sauce or salad dressing, but you control the amount of it you eat. Don't let this decision be made for you by someone in the kitchen who doesn't know you or really care about your health.

* **Don't eat everything on your plate.** I will share a secret with you. I have eaten in restaurants of all types all over the world, and I have never yet been in one where I was forced to eat everything I was served. I think you can safely assume that you are never going to be forced to clean your plate either.

* **Choose low-fat foods.** Nonfat and low-fat foods are available in practically all restaurants, and many now offer "light" alternatives and half portions. If they don't, you may want to order your entree from the appetizer list on the menu.

  Even fast-food restaurants are making it easier for us these days. Some of them have salad bars, and most of them at least have salads available. When they don't, just do the best you can. Scrape some of the sauce off the burger and leave the French fries for someone else.

✳ **Ask the chef to omit what you can't eat.** If broiled fish comes with a rich sauce, you can ask for the fish to be broiled without butter and served without sauce. In a Chinese restaurant ask for your food to be stir-fried in stock or water instead of oil, and request that MSG be omitted. Ask for the skin to be removed from broiled chicken (or remove it yourself). Order the pasta to be served with the vegetables but without the cream sauce. And so on.

✳ **If the menu lists nothing you want, make your own meal from component parts.** If every entree in a Mexican restaurant is dripping with fat, order tortillas, rice, and beans, and roll up your own dish. You can make your own hot salad if you order a large tossed salad and, separately, broiled chicken, fish, or a small steak to put on top. Most restaurants can give you a tossed salad and baked potato, and you can add a little mustard or sauce to the potato for additional flavor. Almost anywhere you go, you should be able to find a way to limit high-fat foods and order something you like. Use your imagination!

Eating Smart When Traveling

I am always amused when readers write to me and explain that they can't possibly control their weight because they have to travel so much and eat out so frequently. I travel over one hundred thousand miles every year, and believe me, I am very familiar with the problems it poses as far as healthful eating is concerned. I finally decided, however, that I was the only one who could do anything about it. It certainly didn't help to complain. The only thing to do is take control of the situation yourself. You are the only one who can truly decide what you will eat and what you won't. You will be delightfully surprised to find out how much more control you have in every situation once you become determined to follow the Eating Smart principles when you're traveling.

Eating Smart in the Air

Flying need not be an experience that routinely throws off your system, and jet lag is not an inevitable result of switching time zones. You've probably heard the standard advice about preparing for a different time zone by going to sleep later or earlier in order to allow your body clock to adjust in advance of a trip. Well, there are several other simple things you can do to ensure a happy landing.

First, drink only nonalcoholic beverages. Avoiding alcoholic beverages is important because the air pressure in an airplane is regulated not to ground level but to around six thousand feet. That causes the effects of alcohol to be much more pronounced in the air. What many people refer to as jet lag is really nothing more than an airborne hangover.

People have told me that they couldn't possibly *not* drink at least one cocktail or a little wine with dinner because they were flying first class, and it seemed dumb not to take advantage of the free drinks. I ask them, "How much more is it costing you to fly first class?" The difference is usually enormous. And, "How much do you think you can drink?" The truth is, when you're flying first class, you're paying for a larger seat, more leg room, and more personal service—not free booze!

Second, drinking lots of water will help prevent dehydration caused by the reduced oxygen in a pressurized cabin. The Pilot's Cocktail (page 33) *does* count as part of your water intake, so it plays a double role, both substituting for a drink and helping you meet your water requirement. You might want to carry a small bottle of angostura bitters with you and make your own Pilot's Cocktail.

Third, eat low-fat meals. Avoiding high-fat foods is even more important while flying than it is on the ground. Fat temporarily inhibits the free flow of oxygen-carrying corpuscles to the brain and robs you of energy, making you feel tired. Eating too much will also make you more uncomfortable in flight than you would be at ground level. This problem is worse when you are at higher altitudes and sitting for long periods of time.

By sticking to these simple rules, you will not only avoid jet lag, you will arrive happy and energized from the flight. Where else can you spend time without outside interruptions such as telephone calls, meetings, and emergencies? Flying provides a wonderful opportunity to plan, work, or just relax and enjoy a good book.

Eating Smart When Traveling on Land

The next time you're planning a trip, ask your travel agent to check the hotels in the cities where you're going to be staying. There may be a hotel that offers an alternative cuisine for its health-conscious guests.

When I travel, I plan ahead for breakfast because I often have to leave a room before room service is available or a restaurant is open. I always pack plastic bags of instant nonfat milk powder, single-serving boxes of shredded wheat, small boxes of raisins, and a spoon. Then, even if I have a very early appointment and have to leave before I can order breakfast, I can mix the milk powder with the water in a glass, add the cereal and raisins, and have a well-balanced meal. The same principles apply for ordering in hotels that we covered earlier in this chapter in the section on restaurants.

As the awareness of the importance of good nutrition grows, so will the availability of nonfat and low-fat dairy products, whole-grain breads, sugar-free and salt-free cereals, and fresh fruit on hotel menus.

AVOID JET LAG

For a happy landing:

* Avoid alcohol.
* Drink a glass of water per hour in flight.
* Avoid fatty foods.
* Eat lightly.

Entertaining

Even though you may be adhering to the Five-to-One Formula menus, what happens when you invite company over for dinner? Everything changes! You're afraid to serve guests what you usually eat for dinner for fear of disappointing them. You feel you have to start with rich high-fat hors d'oeuvres. The crisp, lightly dressed salad will get a heavy Roquefort dressing, the broiled fish or chicken will get a rich sauce, and the vegetables—normally steamed and served without added fat—will be generously coated with butter. Instead of fresh fruit slices for dessert, you'll probably turn the fruit into a pie and then, if the company is really important, serve it à la mode. If you dish out food the way most hosts and hostesses do, you will probably load down your guests' plates with at least twice as much food as they should be eating.

Remember, you are supposed to be entertaining your guests—not trying to kill them!

Instead, plan the menu for your next dinner party as though *you* were going to be the guest. You will be amazed at what a difference this change in thinking makes and how much more your guests will enjoy the meal. You can entertain with great style and imagination and still do it all with Five-to-One Formula menus. Remember Oscar Wilde's great line: "I have the simplest of tastes—I am always satisfied with the best." Five-to-One Formula menu planning *is* the best.

On holidays and other special occasions you don't have to abstain from goodies and treats. You don't have to eat the whole cake to enjoy the party. Moderation, not martyrdom, is the key.

Successful food presentation doesn't need to be time-consuming or require a course in garniture from a culinary institute. Just learning to cut vegetables in different and unusual ways adds a creative touch to your raw vegetable plates and salads. It also makes your cooked vegetables more attractive. For example, the next time you're cutting a carrot, try cutting it on the diagonal instead of just straight across. If you really want to impress your family and friends, make carrot flowers. Several good books about garniture are available. However, just a plate of colorful raw or cold cooked vegetables, such as broccoli, radishes, carrots, jicama, cherry tomatoes, or cauliflower, arranged on a bed of curly lettuce and garnished with sprigs of parsley can look like a photo on the cover of *Gourmet* magazine.

To make your meal appear more special, arrange portions on each plate instead of serving family style. Serving meals in courses not only makes the meal seem more special, it slows down your eating time so that you are satisfied with less food.

Create a pleasant environment with flowers and low lighting or candles. Johns Hopkins Weight Research Program has found that low lighting actually causes you to eat less. Quiet classical music also creates a special ambiance at meal times and helps you to eat more slowly. Other tips for eating slower include using a three-tined instead of a four-tined fork, teaspoons instead of soup spoons for soup, demitasse spoons instead of teaspoons for dessert, and chopsticks.

Eating Smart When You're a Guest

When you're a guest in someone else's home, you face one of the greatest problems the health-conscious person ever experiences in trying to limit fat and calories. Your host or hostess may have the same overindulgent attitude we discussed earlier. He or she may try to make you feel guilty about not finishing some high-fat sauce-laden dish with statements like, "I made it

THE ALLERGIC GUEST

It's always a good idea to inquire about food allergies when inviting people you don't know well for dinner. Recently, I had a dinner party to which I invited someone I knew had an allergy to wheat in any form. I was careful in planning my menu to avoid wheat: I served polenta squares made from cornmeal instead of bread containing wheat, and a flour-free sauce for the salmon.

When the salad was served, one guest couldn't eat it because of the walnuts on it. Another couldn't eat the polenta made from corn. When the salmon was served, I learned of a previously unmentioned fish allergy. Needless to say, I was not a happy hostess!

On the other side of the coin, if you have a food allergy, always let your host or hostess know about it when you are invited—not when you're served.

myself" or, even worse, "I made it just for you." At times like these I always tell my host or hostess how wonderful I think the dish is and ask if I can have the recipe. I go on to explain that I simply can't eat another bite because the hors d'oeuvres were so delicious that I overdid it. But sometimes what I'm really thinking is, "I'm allergic to fat—it keeps my clothes from fitting!"

Speaking of overindulging in appetizers, another pitfall to watch out for is the tendency to eat too many hors d'oeuvres while standing around before dinner. You can end up munching hundreds of calories before you even sit down for the meal. It's advisable to make it a policy not to eat hors d'oeuvres at all or to limit what you eat to raw vegetables. Sipping a glass of water, too, will keep your mouth occupied while waiting for dinner to be served.

Coping with these and other dilemmas you will encounter during those times when you aren't always in complete control of your environment will become easier with practice.

Eating Smart Is Knowing How

Chapter

10

The final step in adapting the Five-to-One Formula to your daily life is reprogramming your thinking and taking control. You now have all the fuel facts. You have all the information necessary for using this strategy, whether you are at home, in a restaurant, entertaining, or a guest in someone else's home. You have learned all the tricks for low-fat cooking and acquired helpful ideas for menu planning. Simply put, you understand why *Eating Smart is knowing how.*

Unlearning the Bad Habits

Armed with all this information, you're ready to make a new start. Doesn't it seem strange that any of us would ever be tempted to live any other way? But the sad fact is that most of us have been conditioned from early childhood not only to run on Limited Fuels but also to overfuel, and to use food as a reward as

129

well as a source of comfort for mental stress and physical pain.

To illustrate exactly how many of us got into this type of situation, I'm going to tell you a fictional story about a man named Sam.

When Sam's parents brought him home from the hospital and he started to cry, how do you think they comforted him? They put a bottle in his mouth! When Sam was old enough to play in his playpen, every time he started to get fussy, someone brought him something to eat to make him happy again. When he got a little older and started to walk, every time he fell down, skinned his knee, and started to cry, can you guess what his parents did? Of course, they ran to him with a cookie or maybe a piece of candy and told him that the "goody" would make everything "all better."

Have you ever seen a parent comfort a child with a carrot stick? Of course not, because we have been conditioned to believe only a "goody" will work. To qualify as a goody, food must contain sugar, fat, or salt, and it's even higher on the goody list if it contains all three.

When Sam was old enough to sit at the table, his preferences were quickly affected by the rest of the family. If left to himself, he probably would never have used salt on his food. Salt is an acquired taste. In fact, if you put salt on a baby's tongue, the baby will start to cry. But Sam saw the other people at the table shaking salt on their food, and so he wanted to do it, too. Before long Sam learned to like salt and to use more and more of it.

Even when Sam wasn't hungry, his parents told him he still had to finish everything on his plate because of all the poor, starving children somewhere in the world. Even worse, they told him he couldn't have dessert until he finished the rest of his meal. The dessert was probably the worst part of the meal from a nutritional standpoint, but it was held out as the reward. Even though Sam was frequently too full to want any more food, he felt he had earned dessert, and he wasn't about to give up his reward—especially if it was chocolate cake!

Not only was dessert held out as a prize for cleaning his plate, but if he was good, Sam could also earn other goodies between meals, such as cookies, candy, and ice cream. On the other hand, if he did something bad, he was punished by not being allowed to have a goody when his brothers and sisters got them. Sam learned not only that you could be rewarded with food when you did something right but also that you could be punished by not getting what you wanted to eat when you did something wrong.

Sam also learned that by eating those goodies he would feel better when he was unhappy or feel even happier on special occasions like Christmas and his birthday.

By the time Sam was a teenager, these eating patterns were normal to him. His life continued to be either feast or famine all the way through high school and college.

Poor Sam, the harder he tried to lose weight, the more obsessed he became with food. When Sam was almost thirty years old, his boss called him into his office and told him that he was so pleased with his work he was going to give him a raise and a big promotion.

Sam was so happy. To celebrate he went out for lunch and had all of his favorite high-fat foods, which he had been denying himself because he was always on some kind of diet. He ordered a roast beef sandwich with gravy and lots of French fries to go with it. He even had chocolate cake for dessert.

About three months later Sam's boss called him into his office and told him he had been disappointed in him since his promotion. He had let the higher salary and the bigger office go to his head, and he was not doing his job. He warned Sam that if he didn't shape up, he was going to be fired.

Sam was depressed, so what did he do? He went out for lunch and had the same gravy-drenched sandwich with French fries that he had eaten to celebrate three months before. Only this time he was eating to make himself feel better. This time he even had a scoop of ice cream to go along with his chocolate cake.

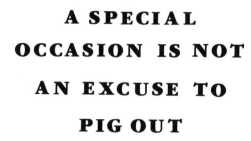

A SPECIAL OCCASION IS NOT AN EXCUSE TO PIG OUT

Do you know how many special occasions there are in every year? In addition to Thanksgiving, Christmas, Hanukkah, Passover, and Easter, there are also Mother's Day, Father's Day, Memorial Day, the Fourth of July, and Valentine's Day—not to mention such personal holidays as birthdays, weddings, anniversaries, christenings, bar mitzvahs, graduations, promotions, and bon voyage parties.

If you were to give yourself permission to eat and drink without limit on every special occasion of the year, you'd end up looking like Santa Claus. Don't fall into the trap of thinking of yourself as a helpless victim of the special occasion or as the beneficiary of a situation in which what you eat doesn't count. Remember that it all counts and that you're just as in control of what you eat on Thanksgiving as you are on any other day of the year.

Sam was in a real Catch-22 situation. Happy or sad, he always thought of food first.

Think how much better off Sam would be today if one of his parents had tried to console him with a new coloring book or a special story instead of a goody when he hurt his knee as a little boy. Or if he had been rewarded with trips to parks or museums instead of cookies or candy when he was especially good. Or if he hadn't been allowed to go to the circus with his brothers and sisters instead of being denied an ice cream cone when he misbehaved. Or if dessert had occasionally been fresh fruit. Or if he had been served smaller portions and not been forced to clean his plate. If . . .

Chances are that as a child you had at least some of the experiences just described. These attitudes toward food are carried over into adulthood. All these unhealthy responses to—and ways of looking at—food were taught to you, and you learned them well. You were not born with these tendencies. They were learned, and they can be unlearned.

For starters, don't buy junk food for yourself or your children. You will have much more success teaching children to snack on healthy food if that's all that's available. You can't very well argue about whether or not your child can have a Ding Dong if there aren't any in the house.

When you're teaching good eating habits to children, it is important not to tell them they can't have dessert unless they finish everything on their plates. When dessert is held out as a reward for eating everything else, most children don't want to give up the reward of dessert even though they are uncomfortably full. They feel they have earned it, and they are somehow going to stuff it in.

Adults display this same attitude learned in childhood when they are too full to enjoy dessert but unwilling to miss having something special. How many times have you been in a restaurant with a friend who said after the meal, "I'm so full. I shouldn't have finished that sandwich," only to perk up when the waiter arrives to ask if you would like to order dessert. Instead of telling the waiter "No, thank you," your friend asks, "What is it?" Isn't this a perfect example of programmed response? In other words, "If it's one of my favorites, I'll somehow manage to cram it in!"

Another mistake parents often make is trying to instill the feeling of guilt in their children for not finishing everything on their plates by reminding them of all of the hungry people in the world.

When one of my sons was still in grammar school, he was invited to have dinner at a friend's house. When I went to pick him up, he looked perplexed. I asked him what was wrong. He told me that his friend's mother had given him too much food and told him he had to eat everything on his plate because of all the poor, starving children. He couldn't understand how it could help other children for him to eat food he didn't want. I told him that if it ever happened again, he could politely ask his friend's mother to wrap up the extra food and send it to them.

Well, he couldn't wait to get back there for dinner. Even if he had been ravenously hungry, I'm sure he wouldn't have eaten much just so he could ask the mother to wrap up the food! But, of course, he prefaced it with, "My mother said . . ."

Thank heavens this woman had a good sense of humor. She called me the next day and said, "Thank you. I never realized how ridiculous I was being. My parents always told me I had to finish everything on my plate because of all the poor, starving children, and I just figured that was the way to teach children not to waste food."

You are not going to keep from "wasting" food that is already on your plate by eating it. *Stop* when you are no longer hungry. If you don't eat it, it will go into the garbage disposal and end up in the city's central sewage system. If you do eat it, it will eventually end up in the same place. You will look better, feel better, and probably live longer if you process it through the garbage disposal and not your body!

All the bad habits learned in childhood can be corrected in adulthood. We can actually be reprogrammed, and we can do it ourselves.

Managing Your Body

At a time when so much emphasis is being placed on sound business management practices and increased productivity, why not treat managing your own body the same way a good manager would treat any other management problem? First you define the problem, which is obvious if you're overweight, and then you take the necessary steps to correct the problem.

One thing that makes good body management unique is that there isn't anyone, including yourself, who can argue that the problem should not be solved. Also, the solution to the problem will cost you nothing. In fact, as pointed out earlier, it will save you money not only in food bills but also in medical bills. What an enviable management solution!

Here are a few suggestions:

* **Look at what you're eating.** Before you start to eat, take a good look at your plate. How much of it is on the Preferred Fuel list we discussed earlier (page 70)? How much of it is coming primarily from the Limited Fuels lists (page 74)? Does your meal look as if it fits the Five-to-One Formula?
* **Set your goals and make them realistic.** You put the weight on gradually, and it must come off the same way. A loss of one or two pounds a week is generally considered safe.
* **Make lists.** Good managers know the importance of keeping lists. Keeping a food diary may be helpful, especially in the beginning. Also, make a list of the things you're going to do in your free time, things that will help you take your mind off eating when you're not really hungry but simply bored.
* **Reduce stress.** In our jet age there is more and more need for planned relaxation. Even just a few minutes away

from concentrated effort—some deep breathing or stretching—will help. If you sit at a computer terminal, relaxation is especially important for the nerves as well as the eyes.

❋ **Get enough rest.** Getting an adequate amount of sleep is necessary for good health. Everyone's needs are different, but Eating Smart will help you sleep so soundly that you may require less sleep. Then you will have more waking hours for other activities.

❋ **Never skip breakfast.** This applies even if you had too much to eat the night before. It's a crutch used by many compulsive night eaters, and it doesn't work.

❋ **Stop eating when you are no longer hungry.** If you continue to eat until you have that bloated, uncomfortable feeling caused by overeating, you will start to feel guilty and out of control rather than proud of yourself. When you're proud of yourself, you don't overeat. And vice versa.

For some strange reason that behavioral psychologists have never been able to explain, it is also this feeling of discomfort from overeating that triggers a binge of compulsive eating. You are much more likely to raid the refrigerator when you come home from a party or a meal in a restaurant uncomfortably full and feeling guilty about it.

The obvious solution is not to continue eating when you are no longer hungry. If you do, don't feel guilty, feel human. We can all learn from our mistakes. Don't berate yourself, you already feel miserable enough. The only way to get right back on track is to return to the Five-to-One Formula the next meal.

Remember, you're not on a diet, you're on a lifelong program of Eating Smart.

❋ **Exercise.** A good way to counter the impulse to overeat is to plan to exercise about thirty minutes after each meal. Stop eating while you still feel like doing some form of physical activity. Another positive result of exercising after meals is that the elevated metabolic rate that always results from eating is further raised by exercising.

Remember, the positive advantages of increased metabolism are maintained for many hours afterward. Any form of exercise will do. Go for a walk, take a bicycle ride, play tennis, swim, dance, or make love. The important thing is to do something besides just sit and get fat.

✳ **Slow down!** The slower you eat, the smaller the amount of food it takes to satisfy your appetite. Your brain can't tell that you are no longer hungry until your blood sugar has risen sufficiently to trigger a brain response. If you are wolfing your food down as fast as you can, you will almost certainly eat too much.

There are many classic behavioral suggestions for slowing the rate at which you consume food. Some of them were mentioned earlier, such as dividing meals into several courses and using a three-tined instead of a four-tined fork. There are many others as well: eating consciously by enjoying each bite to its fullest, chewing each bite a prescribed number of times, and putting your fork down between bites. Don't combine snacking with any other activities such as watching television, reading, or playing cards.

All of these techniques work for different people at different times. My advice is to use any or all of them that help you.

✳ **Don't use drugs.** Never try to manage your weight with diet or weight-loss drugs, whether they are prescription drugs or the over-the-counter variety. According to Dr. Marc Shuckett, a professor of psychiatry at the University of California at San Diego School of Medicine, all weight-loss pills are addictive drugs that fall into the category of stimulants. Among other drugs in this category are cocaine and amphetamines.

Weight-loss drugs are dangerous and don't work.

Weight-loss pills are attractive drugs because they make you feel more energetic and suppress your appetite—but only in the beginning. Then it takes larger and larger doses to achieve the same effect because your body builds up a tolerance to the drug. When you start taking larger doses, you feel nervous. Your blood pressure goes up. You may even feel heart palpitations; some people think they are having heart attacks and rush to the hospital. In extreme cases of diet pill overdose, the heart can even start beating so fast that it stops, causing death.

After you stop taking the drug, you will experience a rebound reaction. The withdrawal symptoms of any addictive drug are the same: the exact opposite of the effects you experienced when you first started taking the drug. So instead of feeling energetic and on top of the world, you are constantly tired and depressed. Instead of not having much appetite, you are constantly hungry and obsessed with food. You will gain back more weight than you lost in the first place.

✱ **Don't go by the numbers.** Compulsively jumping on the scales every morning and letting the numbers you read dictate your mood for the day is *not* the way to manage your eating behavior. You never judge other people by those numbers, so why judge yourself that way? Can you imagine seeing an attractive woman walking across a room and thinking, "Great figure, about a hundred and twenty-five pounds." Of course not. We all judge other people's bodies by the way they look. So why not apply this same principle to your own body?

If weighing yourself every day served any useful purpose it would be different, but it doesn't. In fact, it's counterproductive. You don't take into account the normal fluctuations in body fluids that affect your weight on a daily basis. It can give you a false sense of satisfaction or lead to unnecessary anxiety. You're trying to lose weight only to find you have gained two pounds. Guess what happens to your behavior? You are discouraged and unhappy with yourself, so you eat more all day long.

Another problem with scale weight is that it doesn't tell you what percentage of your weight is muscle and what percentage is fat. Muscle weighs more than fat. The higher the percentage of muscle you have relative to the percentage of fat, the better your metabolism is. The better your metabolism is, the more calories you burn up every day. Therefore, a higher metabolism means that you can take in more fuel every day and still maintain your desired weight.

Instead of jumping on the scale, stand stark naked in front of a full-length mirror. This will tell you how you really look. This body management project doesn't require any charts or graphs. When your clothes start fitting again and you start feeling more enthusiastic about life in general, you'll know your management plan is working. However, if you want to keep a record of the progress you are making in the pursuit of a better body, do it with a tape measure and a log of your measurements each week or month—not a scale!

Putting It All Together

Many people don't know what it's like to feel good. They have been trudging along on inferior fuels for so long that they think the way they feel is normal. If you are in this category, prepare yourself, because after a week of following the Eating Smart program you are going to experience a new natural high that is so euphoric you may well wonder what is wrong with you. Actually, everything is right with you, so enjoy your newfound energy and fantastic feeling of well-being.

This feeling is addictive. Once you've experienced the euphoria caused by Eating Smart and getting an adequate amount of exercise, you'll never be able to give it up. In fact, you will be anxious to spread the word—to share your knowledge about Eating Smart with your family and friends.

* Eat five times more carbohydrate foods than animal protein foods.
* Limit fat.
* Drink at least eight glasses of water every day.
* Use sugar and salt sparingly.
* Consume alcoholic beverages only in moderation.
* Get enough exercise.
* . . . and smile!

Appendix
A Few Basic Recipes

On the following pages are a few recipes that demonstrate how to cook practically fat-free and still enjoy foods that are low in calories and fat, and high in appeal. I've included several salad dressings, some spreads and sauces, soup recipes, and a few sample lunch or dinner dishes, along with examples of desserts and beverages.

Fifteen-Minute Chicken Stock

3–5 pounds chicken bones, parts, and giblets, excluding the liver
2 carrots, scraped and chopped
2 stalks celery, without leaves, chopped
1 onion, unpeeled, quartered
3 parsley sprigs
2 to 4 cloves garlic, unpeeled, halved
1 bay leaf
12 peppercorns
¼ cup vinegar
Cold water to cover by 1 inch

Put all the ingredients into a large pot with a lid. Add cold water to cover and bring slowly to a boil. Preparation to this point takes about 5 minutes.

Reduce the heat, cover, leaving lid ajar, and simmer for 3 hours or more. Longer cooking makes the stock more flavorful. Remove from the heat and allow to stand until cool enough to handle. Remove the chicken parts and vegetables and discard. Strain the stock and cool to room temperature. This second step takes 5 minutes more. Refrigerate, uncovered, overnight or until the fat has congealed on top.

Remove the fat and store the stock in the freezer in containers of a volume you most often use. This final step completes the 15 minutes of preparation time.

Makes approximately 10 cups (2½ quarts)

1 cup contains approximately:

Calories:	Negligible
Cholesterol:	Negligible
Fat:	Negligible
Sodium:	Varies

Fat-Free Dressing

½ cup red wine vinegar
½ teaspoon salt
¼ teaspoon freshly ground black pepper
1 tablespoon sugar
2 garlic cloves, minced

2 teaspoons Worcestershire sauce
1 tablespoon Dijon mustard
1 tablespoon fresh lemon juice
1 cup water

Combine vinegar and salt and stir until salt is completely dissolved. Add all other ingredients except water and mix well. Add water and again mix well. Refrigerate.

Makes 2 cups

Each 2-tablespoon serving contains approximately:

Calories:	5
Cholesterol:	0 mg
Fat:	Negligible
Sodium:	117 mg

Variations:
Italian Dressing: Using a mortar and pestle, crush together 1 teaspoon each of dried leaf oregano, basil, and tarragon, and add it to the dressing.

Mexican Dressing: Add ½ teaspoon of ground cumin.

Oriental Dressing: Add 1 teaspoon of curry powder and ⅛ teaspoon of ground ginger (optional).

Tarragon Dressing: Add 1 tablespoon of dried leaf tarragon, crushed with a mortar and pestle.

Hot Mushroom Fat-Free Dressing

1 pound fresh mushrooms, ¾ cup Fat-Free Dressing (see
   sliced (4 cups)   recipe on page 144)

Combine mushrooms and dressing in a skillet and cook until
the mushrooms are just tender, about 5 minutes.

Makes 4 (½-cup) servings

Each serving contains approximately:

Calories: 32
Cholesterol: 0 mg
Fat: Negligible
Sodium: 132 mg

Creamy Curry Dressing

1 pint silken soft tofu   1½ teaspoons curry powder
   (1 pound)   ¼ teaspoon ginger
1 teaspoon salt   4 teaspoons fresh lemon juice
2 teaspoons sugar

Combine all ingredients in a blender and blend until smooth.
Chill for several hours before use.

Makes 2 cups

1 tablespoon contains approximately:

Calories: 10
Cholesterol: 0 mg
Fat: Negligible
Sodium: 56 mg

▰▰

Thousand Island Dressing

1 cup reduced-calorie
 mayonnaise
½ cup bottled chili sauce
¼ cup sweet pickle relish
2 tablespoons white vinegar

¼ teaspoon salt
½ teaspoon sugar
Dash of freshly ground black
 pepper
1 tablespoon fresh lemon
 juice

Combine all ingredients in a medium bowl and mix thoroughly.
Refrigerate in a tightly covered container.

Makes 2 scant cups

2 tablespoons contains approximately:

Calories: 35
Cholesterol: 0
Fat: 2 g
Sodium: 80 mg

▄▄

Raspberry Walnut Vinaigrette Dressing

½ cup raspberry vinegar
¼ teaspoon salt
3 cups water
Pinch of freshly ground black pepper
1 tablespoon sugar
2 garlic cloves, minced
1½ teaspoons Worcestershire sauce

1½ teaspoons Dijon mustard
1 tablespoon fresh lemon juice
1 tablespoon dried leaf tarragon, crushed using mortar and pestle
2 tablespoons walnut oil

Combine the vinegar and salt, and stir until the salt has dissolved. Add all the other ingredients except the oil and mix well.

Add oil and again mix well.

Store, covered, in the refrigerator. Always mix well before serving.

Makes 2 cups

Each 2-tablespoon serving contains approximately:

Calories:	15
Cholesterol:	0
Fat:	Negligible
Sodium:	188 mg

Variations:
You can use this recipe as a basis for many others simply by changing the type of vinegar and oil you use. Try using tarragon vinegar and extra-virgin olive oil, or come up with your own special "house" dressing.

Mayo-Not

This is not a bread spread but an excellent substitute for mayonnaise in recipes.

½ pound tofu, cubed (1 cup)   1 tablespoon freshly
1 tablespoon canola or olive   squeezed lemon juice
                          oil   ½ teaspoon salt

Place all ingredients in a blender and blend until smooth. Refrigerate in a tightly covered container. It will keep one week.

Makes 1 cup

Each ¼-cup serving contains approximately:

Calories:	75
Cholesterol:	0 mg
Fat:	6 g
Sodium:	281 mg

━━
Mustard Sauce

1 cup Mayo-Not (see recipe, page 148)
2 tablespoons Dijon-style mustard
¼ teaspoon dried thyme, crushed in a mortar with a pestle
¼ teaspoon dried rosemary, crushed in a mortar with a pestle
⅛ teaspoon freshly ground black pepper
1 clove garlic, quartered

Combine all ingredients in a blender and blend until satin-smooth. Refrigerate in a tightly covered container.

Makes about 1 cup

Each tablespoon contains approximately:

Calories:	18
Cholesterol:	0 mg
Fat:	2 g
Sodium:	51 mg

━━
Fat-Free Gravy

This recipe works for any kind of gravy. Adjust the seasonings as you wish. For more flavor sauté some chopped onion in a little of the drippings before proceeding with the recipe.

1 cup de-fatted beef drippings (saved from roasting pan, etc.)	2 tablespoons cornstarch or arrowroot
1 cup de-fatted beef stock	¼ cup water
	Salt, to taste

Heat the beef drippings and beef stock in a saucepan. Mix the cornstarch or arrowroot with the water and add to the stock mixture. Cook over medium heat, stirring occasionally, until thickened. Add salt to taste.

Makes 1 to 1½ cups

¼ cup contains approximately:

Calories:	Negligible
Cholesterol:	Negligible
Fat:	Negligible
Sodium:	Varies

Marinade

1½ tablespoons oregano, crushed in a mortar with a pestle	4 cloves garlic, minced
4 bay leaves, crushed	½ cup sodium-reduced soy sauce
½ teaspoon freshly ground black pepper	2 cups sweet vermouth
¼ cup red wine vinegar	2 cups dry sherry
	2 tablespoons canola oil

Combine all ingredients and mix thoroughly. Marinate the meat of your choice all day or overnight in the refrigerator. Marinades add only negligible amounts of calories, fat, and sodium.

Makes about 4 cups

Breakfast Cheese

1 cup (8 ounces) part-skim ricotta cheese	2 tablespoons plain nonfat yogurt

Combine the ricotta cheese and yogurt in a food processor with a metal blade and blend until satiny-smooth.

Refrigerate in a tightly covered container. The fresher your ingredients, the longer you'll be able to store breakfast cheese.

Makes about 1 cup

Each 2-tablespoon serving contains approximately:

Calories:	40
Cholesterol:	9 mg
Fat:	2 g
Sodium:	38 mg

Yogurt Sauce

1 cup plain nonfat yogurt	½ teaspoon ground cinnamon
1 teaspoon vanilla extract	

Combine all ingredients and mix thoroughly. Cover and refrigerate.

Makes 1 cup

2 tablespoons contains approximately:

Calories:	23
Cholesterol:	1 mg
Fat:	0 g
Sodium:	40 mg

Apple Butter

¼ pound dried unsulfured sliced apples (2 cups)

1 teaspoon ground cinnamon

½ teaspoon ground allspice

⅛ teaspoon ground cloves

2 cups unsweetened apple juice

Combine all ingredients in a large saucepan and bring to a boil. Lower the heat and simmer, covered, for 20 minutes, stirring occasionally. Remove from the heat and cool slightly.

Pour into a blender or food processor and blend until smooth. Cool to room temperature, then refrigerate in a tightly covered container. It will keep for months.

Makes 2 cups

Each 2-tablespoon serving contains approximately:

Calories:	35
Cholesterol:	0 mg
Fat:	Negligible
Sodium:	5 mg

Marinara Sauce

2 medium onions finely chopped (3 cups)
2 garlic cloves, minced
5 cups tomato sauce
2½ cups water
1 teaspoon dried oregano, crushed with a mortar and pestle
1 teaspoon dried basil, crushed with a mortar and pestle
¼ teaspoon dried thyme, crushed with a mortar and pestle
¼ teaspoon dried rosemary, crushed with a mortar and pestle
1 bay leaf, broken
½ teaspoon salt
½ teaspoon sugar
¼ teaspoon freshly ground black pepper
⅛ teaspoon cayenne pepper

Cook the onions and garlic in a heavy skillet, covered, over very low heat until they are soft. Add a little water if necessary to prevent scorching.

Add all other ingredients and bring to a boil. Lower the heat and simmer, uncovered, for at least 2 hours.

Makes 4 cups, eight ½-cup servings

Each serving contains approximately:

Calories:	70
Cholesterol:	0 mg
Fat:	Negligible
Sodium:	1,060 mg

■■

Dried Onion Soup Mix

Many recipes call for dried onion soup. Since commercial preparations are high in sodium, you might want to try this low-sodium version instead.

½ teaspoon onion powder	¼ teaspoon Kitchen Bouquet
½ teaspoon salt	Browning Sauce
¼ teaspoon sugar	½ cup chopped or minced
	dehydrated onion

Combine the onion powder, salt, and sugar in a small bowl. Add the Kitchen Bouquet and stir until the seasonings are uniformly brown. Add the dehydrated onion and mix thoroughly until the color is again even. (This step takes several minutes.)

Makes ½ cup
Note: equivalent to one (1½-ounce) envelope of dried onion soup mix.

Each 1-tablespoon serving contains approximately:

Calories:	12
Cholesterol:	0 mg
Fat:	0 g
Sodium:	149 mg

■■

Cream of Mushroom Soup

Use this soup in any recipe that calls for cream of mushroom soup. It's lower in fat and calories than commercial preparations.

1 tablespoon corn oil margarine
3 tablespoons unbleached flour
¾ cup defatted chicken stock
½ cup skim milk
¼ teaspoon salt (omit if using salted stock)
Dash of garlic powder
Dash of freshly ground black pepper
¼ cup freshly cooked or canned mushrooms, finely chopped

Melt the margarine in a skillet. Add the flour and stir over medium heat for 1 minute. Do not brown. Add the chicken stock and skim milk. Using a wire whisk, stir the mixture over medium heat until it comes to a boil. Add the seasonings and mushrooms, and continue to cook for 1 minute more. To serve as soup, dilute to taste with water, stock, or skim milk.

Makes 1¼ cups

1¼ cups contains approximately:

Calories:	250
Cholesterol:	2 mg
Fat:	12 g
Sodium:	625 mg

Variations:
Cream of Chicken Soup: Omit the mushrooms and add ¼ cup of finely chopped cooked chicken.

Cream of Celery Soup: Omit the mushrooms and add ¼ cup of finely chopped celery.

Vegetable Bisque

This recipe for a basic vegetable bisque uses zucchini, but any vegetable will work. Try broccoli, carrots, tomatoes, or any vegetable you have left over.

½ onion, chopped
3 medium zucchini, chopped
1½ cups Fifteen Minute Chicken Stock (see recipe, page 143)

¼ teaspoon salt (omit if using salted stock)
¼ teaspoon curry powder
¼ cup plain low-fat yogurt

Combine the onion, zucchini, and chicken stock in a pot and bring to a boil. Lower the heat and cook, covered, for 10 minutes.

Spoon the mixture into a blender. Add all the other ingredients and blend until smooth. Serve hot or cold.

Makes 3 cups

Each ½-cup serving contains approximately:

Calories:	25
Cholesterol:	1 mg
Fat:	Negligible
Sodium:	108 mg

Canyon Ranch Stuffed Spud

2 small baking potatoes
1 medium onion, finely
chopped
¼ cup buttermilk
½ cup low-fat cottage cheese

3 tablespoons grated
Parmesan or Romano
cheese
2 tablespoons chopped green
onions, including the tops

Wash the potatoes well. Pierce with a fork and bake at 400°F for 1 hour.

Cut a very thin slice from the top of each potato. Remove the pulp from the potatoes, being careful not to tear the shells. Mash the potato pulp and set aside in a covered bowl. Keep the shells warm.

Cook the onion over low heat, covered, until soft, stirring occasionally to prevent scorching. Add the mashed potatoes and remaining ingredients except the chopped green onions. Mix well and heat thoroughly. Stuff the potato mixture back into the warm shells; it should heap over the top of the shells.

To serve, sprinkle the top of each stuffed spud with 1 tablespoon of chopped green onion. If you have prepared them in advance, heat in a 350°F oven for 10 to 15 minutes, or until hot, before adding the chopped onions.

Makes 2 servings

Each serving contains approximately:

Calories:	342
Cholesterol:	12 mg
Fat:	4 g
Sodium:	419 mg

Bean Burritos

5½ cups Refried Beans (see   8 whole wheat flour tortillas
following recipe)

Heat the beans and tortillas. Spoon ⅔ cup of the bean mixture onto the lower half of each tortilla. Fold each tortilla like an envelope around the beans.

Makes 8 servings

Each serving contains approximately:

Calories:	248
Cholesterol:	0 mg
Fat:	3 g
Sodium:	60 mg

Refried Beans

½ medium onion, chopped (¾ cup)
1 clove garlic, minced
1½ cups dried pinto beans that have been soaked overnight
½ teaspoon freshly ground black pepper

2 quarts water or to cover
1 teaspoon salt (optional)
2½ cups chopped onion
2 cups chopped tomatoes
1 tablespoon finely chopped cilantro
¼ cup chopped green chiles
½ teaspoon cumin
1½ teaspoons chili powder

Combine onion and garlic in a heavy pot and cook, covered, over low heat until soft, about 10 minutes. Add a little water if necessary to prevent scorching. Drain and rinse the beans. Add them along with the pepper to the onions and garlic. Cover with water and bring to a boil. Reduce heat and simmer over medium heat, covered, for 2½ to 3½ hours, until the beans are tender. Add additional boiling water if needed.

When the beans are tender, stir in the salt. Store in the refrigerator until needed or continue with the recipe.

Drain the beans, reserving 1 cup of broth. Place the beans in a food processor and process until they are the consistency of refried beans. Add broth if necessary.

In a large, heavy pan, cook the 2½ cups of chopped onion and the tomatoes over low heat until soft. Add the beans, cilantro, green chiles, cumin, and chili powder. Cook over medium heat, stirring occasionally, until the liquid is reduced and the beans do not run when spooned onto a plate.

Makes 5½ cups

⅔ cup contains approximately:

Calories:	148
Cholesterol:	0 mg
Fat:	Negligible
Sodium:	10 mg

Vegetable Stew

Beans:

½ cup small white beans that have been soaked overnight and drained
1 onion, peeled and stuck with 2 cloves
1 carrot, peeled and quartered
½ teaspoon salt
¼ teaspoon freshly ground black pepper
½ teaspoon thyme, crushed with a mortar and pestle
½ teaspoon rosemary, crushed with a mortar and pestle

Vegetables:

2 medium turnips, peeled and cubed
2 medium potatoes, peeled and cubed
2 stalks celery, sliced into ¼-inch crescents
3 large carrots, peeled and sliced in ½-inch rounds
4 leeks, white part only, sliced
¼ head medium cabbage, shredded
5 cups water
1 teaspoon salt
¼ teaspoon freshly ground black pepper
1 teaspoon crushed thyme (using a mortar and pestle)
1 teaspoon crushed rosemary (using a mortar and pestle)
Finely chopped parsley for garnish (optional)

To prepare the beans, combine all the ingredients, cover with water, and bring to a boil. Lower the heat to simmer and cook until the beans are tender, about 2 hours. Drain the beans and discard the onion and carrot.

While the beans are cooking, prepare the vegetables. Combine the turnips, potatoes, celery, carrots, leeks, and cabbage with 1 cup of the water in a large pot or soup kettle. Cook over low heat, covered, until the vegetables are tender, about 30 minutes. Do not brown!

Add the drained beans to the vegetables. Add the remaining 4 cups of water, salt, pepper, thyme, and rosemary. Bring to a boil, lower the heat, and simmer, covered, for 30 minutes. Remove from the heat and allow to cool slightly. Remove 4 cups of the vegetables and puree. Pour the pureed vegetables back into the stew and mix well. Heat to the desired temperature.

To serve, ladle 1½ cups of stew into a bowl or soup plate. Top with chopped parsley, if desired.

Makes 12 cups, eight 1½-cup servings

Each serving contains approximately:

Calories:	185
Cholesterol:	0 mg
Fat:	5 g
Sodium:	665 mg

Linguine with Clam Sauce

½ pound dry linguine (4 cups cooked)
1 (8-ounce) can chopped clams, undrained

1 clove garlic, minced
2 ounces imported Parmesan cheese, grated (½ cup)

Cook the linguine according to the package directions until *al dente* or slightly resistant to the bite.

Heat the clams in their juice along with the garlic until heated through. *Do not boil.*

Drain the pasta, toss with the clam and garlic mixture, and the grated Parmesan cheese. Serve on heated plates.

Makes 4 servings

Each serving contains approximately:

Calories:	250
Cholesterol:	55 mg
Fat:	5 g
Sodium:	265 mg

Garbanzo Nuts

1 pound garbanzo beans that
have been soaked
overnight and drained
Water

1 onion, peeled and
quartered
¼ cup low-sodium soy sauce

Put the drained beans in a heavy pot and add water to cover by 3 inches. Add onion and soy sauce. Bring to a boil, lower the heat, and simmer for 1 hour, or until the beans are tender.

Preheat the oven to 350°F. Drain the cooked beans and remove the onion. Spray 2 baking pans with nonstick vegetable spray. Spread the beans in the pans in a single layer. Place the pans in the oven and bake for 1 hour, or until crisp and crunchy, stirring occasionally so that they will brown evenly. (Or bake for 50 minutes, turn the oven off, and leave the beans in the oven until cool.)

Each ¼ cup contains approximately:

Calories:	52
Cholesterol:	0 mg
Fat:	1 g
Sodium:	100 mg

Pumpkin Mousse

1 (16-ounce) carton part-skim ricotta cheese
2 cups mashed cooked pumpkin
3 tablespoons sugar
1 tablespoon ground cinnamon
1 teaspoon allspice
⅛ teaspoon mace
1½ tablespoons vanilla extract

Combine all ingredients in a food processor with a metal blade and blend until satiny-smooth.

Refrigerate until cold. Place ½ cup of mousse in each dish.

Makes 12 servings

½ cup contains approximately:

Calories:	91
Cholesterol:	13 mg
Fat:	3 g
Sodium:	54 mg

Cherry Trifle

2 cups nonfat milk	8 ounces angel food cake, cut
2 tablespoons cornstarch	in 1-inch cubes (4 cups)
⅓ cup sugar	6 tablespoons sherry
4 egg whites, lightly beaten	1½ pounds frozen
2 teaspoons canola oil	unsweetened pitted dark
1½ teaspoons vanilla extract	cherries, thawed (3 cups)

Combine the milk and cornstarch in a saucepan and mix until the cornstarch is completely dissolved. Add the sugar, egg whites, and oil. Mix well and bring slowly to a boil, stirring constantly with a wire whisk until thickened. Remove from the heat, stir in the vanilla extract, and allow the custard to cool to room temperature.

To assemble the trifle, place ⅓ of the cake pieces in the bottom of a 2-quart glass bowl or trifle dish. Sprinkle with 2 tablespoons of sherry, then spoon ⅔ cup of custard evenly over the cake. Spoon 1 cup of cherries over the custard. Repeat the process two more times, then cover and refrigerate. Serve chilled.

Makes twelve ¾-cup servings

Each serving contains approximately:

Calories	143
Cholesterol:	1 mg
Fat:	1 g
Sodium:	93 mg

▄▀
Banana-Bran Shake

1 cup nonfat milk   ½ frozen banana*
⅓ cup uncooked oat bran,

Combine all ingredients in a blender and blend until smooth.

Makes one 1½-cup serving

Each serving contains approximately:

Calories:	215
Cholesterol:	4 mg
Fat:	3 g
Sodium:	131 mg

*To freeze bananas, peel and store them in tightly sealed bags or containers in your freezer.

▄▀
Sugar-Free White Eggnog

1 egg   1 teaspoon vanilla extract
¾ cup skim milk   ¼ teaspoon rum extract
1 tablespoon frozen   2 ice cubes, crushed
unsweetened apple juice   Ground nutmeg or cinnamon
concentrate   for garnish

Dip the whole egg, in its shell, in boiling water for 30 seconds. Break open the egg and put the white only in a blender.

Add the milk, apple juice concentrate, vanilla and rum extracts, and ice cubes, and blend until smooth and frothy. Pour into a large glass and sprinkle with nutmeg or cinnamon.

Makes 1 serving

Each serving contains approximately:

Calories:	125
Cholesterol:	3 mg
Fat:	1 g
Sodium:	220 mg

Subject Index

Aerobic exercises, 51–53
Alcohol, 76; calories and, 30, 32, 34; nonalcoholic alternatives, 33; on plane trips, 122
Allergies, 127
"All natural" foods, 66
Ambiance at meal times, 126
Amino acids, 6, 11
Animal protein, 9–11, 70–71, 74, 77
Appetizers, overindulging in, 128
Avocado oil, 17

Bananas, 63; for beverages, 106; with pancakes, 113–14; storage of, 68
Beans. *See* Legumes
Beard, James, 100
Beef. *See* Meat
Beer, 32, 34
Beverages: fat-free, 106; limited fuels (group A), 76; limited fuels (group B), 78–79; preferred fuels, 73. *See also* Alcohol
Blood sugar, 9, 32
Breads: storage of, 69. *See also* Grain products
Breakfast: menu planning for, 111–14; skipping of, 47–48, 136; traveling and, 123
Brioche rolls, 31
Brody, Jane, 66–67
Butter, 14, 31

Caffeine, 22–23
Calcium, 27
Calories, 29, 30; alcohol and, 30, 32, 34; daily needs, 45; density concerns, 30–32; fats and, 30–32, 38–39; limiting of, 34, 35–37 (*see also* Five-to-One Formula); sources of, 29–30

Canned goods, 72, 79

Canola oil, 17

Carbohydrates, 6; calories and, 30; complex, 7, 70; limited fuels (group A), 74; limited fuels (group B), 77; preferred fuels, 70; simple, 7, 9

Catsup, 79

Cereals. *See* Grain products

Ceviche, 87

Cheese. *See* Dairy products

Chicken. *See* Poultry

Cholesterol, 16; in eggs, 11; fiber and, 8; "good" and "bad," 17, 16; grapefruit and, 111–12; problems caused by, 16; saturated fats and, 14–15

Chromium, 27

Cinnamon, 90

Clothing when cooking, 83

Cocoa, 14, 79

Coconut, 14, 15

Coffee, 22–23, 76, 78

Cold boxes, 115

Condiments: limited fuels (group A), 76; limited fuels (group B), 79; preferred fuels, 73

Cooking light, 81–82; altering recipes for, 107; basic techniques, 82, 84–86; beverages, 106; clothing for, 83; egg whites for, 85–86; fish preparation, 86–87; herbs for seasoning, 93–94; legume preparation, 104; meat preparation, 89; milk for, 85; pasta preparation, 104–5; potato preparation, 99–101; poultry preparation, 87–88; salad preparation, 101–2, 104; salt and, 91–93; snacks, 106–7; sugar and, 90–91; vegetable preparation, 94–104

Cooper, Kenneth, 58

Copper, 27

Corn oil, 15

Cottonseed oil, 15

Croissants, 31

Dairy products: limited fuels (group A), 74; limited fuels (group B), 77; preferred fuels, 71; protein and, 10; storage of, 67. *See also* Eggs; Milk

Desserts, 91, 101; attitudes about, 130–31, 133–34

Dieting. *See* Weight management

Diet sodas, 79

Digestion, 52

Dinner menu planning, 116–17

Drippings, fat-free, 84–85

Drugs for losing weight, 137–38

Eggs, 112–13; cholesterol and, 11; for cooking, 85–86; protein and, 10, 11; saturated fats and, 14. *See also* Dairy products

Employee exercise programs, 60

Entertaining, 125–26, 127

Exercise, 48; aerobics, 51–53; after meals, 52, 136–37; benefits of, 49; daily habit of, 59–60; enjoyment factor, 50; pacing yourself, 52, 58; personal program for, 60; stretching, 53–58; time for daily exercise, 50; travel and, 60; walking, 59; warming up and cooling down, 52

Fast-food restaurants, 120

"Fat free" foods, 66

Fats, 6, 13–15; body's production of, 6; calories and, 30–32, 38–39; limited fuels (group A), 75–76; limited fuels (group B), 78; limiting fats in diet, 34–37 (*see also* Five-to-One Formula); low-fat cooking (*see* Cooking light); in

Recipe Index

Recipe Index